All Fall Down
The Brandon deWilde Story

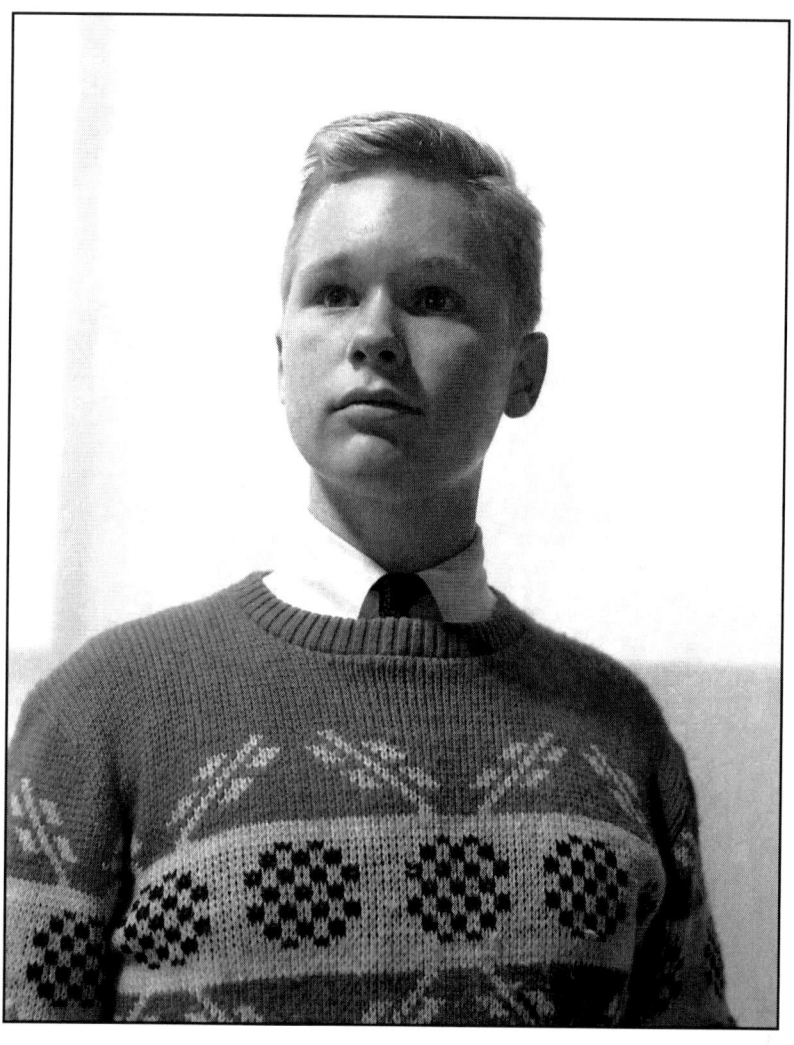

by *Patrisha Mc Lean*

All Fall Down
The Brandon deWilde Story

©2013 Faces Inc.
Second edition, revised

ISBN 13: 978-1-938883-41-5

All rights reserved. No part of this book may be reproduced in any form or by any electronic or mechanical means, including information storage and retrieval systems, without permission in writing from the author, except by a reviewer, who may quote brief passages in review.

Cover design by Marcie Jan Bronstein

Printed by Maine Authors Publishing
558 Main Street, Rockland, Maine 04841
www.maineauthorspublishing.com

Manufactured in the United States of America

To Janice, for trusting me.

Contents

1. A boy who will melt your heart 5
2. Members of the whole world. 11
3. Golden boy. 23
4. Going places. 39
5. A class act. 47
6. King of the child stars 83
7. Growing up 93
8. Music Man. 103
9. All grown up 111
10. There goes the movie star 117
11. Member of the band 127
12. So you wanna be a rock 'n roll star 161
13. Wild in the sky 171
14. Janice 179
15. Butterflies are free 189

Photo Gallery #1. 57
Photo Gallery #2. 135
Acknowledgements 200
Bibliography 203
Career Credits 204

Author's Note

When my husband and I were newlyweds, I showed him the movie *The Member of the Wedding*, and he showed me *Shane*, on a 16 mm film projector with films ordered from the then-thriving, now-defunct catalogue the Big Reel. And we both fell in love anew with the tow-headed, gap-toothed boy who starred in both. Wanting to know what happened to Brandon deWilde, and finding scant material, I slipped back into my premarital newspaper reporter mode and set about to uncover his story myself.

I finished the manuscript, with Brandon's last two years remaining sketchy because I was stymied in locating, or even finding anything about, Janice Gero, the second wife who lived with him during this period. Then ensued a long period of roller coaster dealings with agents and publishers. I put the manuscript aside and turned my energy to a career as a photographer specializing in black and white portraits of children.

When I finally heeded my daughter's nagging and dug the manuscript out of storage, I was shocked at how much time had gone by. Jackie Lee wasn't born when I did my original research and is now a college senior (and writer herself). Also in the interim, the internet had exploded and a bounty of fresh material about Brandon was now available on the exemplary website RememberingBrandon.net. Alas, though, still no light on my subject's last two years.

Just as I was planning to send my manuscript to the printer, the contact information for the elusive Janice was e-mailed to me from a priest in Italy, who read about my upcoming book on the RememberingBrandon website.

In the many phone conversations with Janice that followed, she recounted with warmth and candor remarkable for the sensitivity of the subject, finding the love of her life at nineteen, marrying him at twenty-one, and losing him three months later.

"Talk about preproduction," said Peppy Castro, a musician friend of Brandon's, when I let him know that the book was coming out. A priest, a dedicated fan and webmaster, and a devoted widow, made the wait worthwhile.

Brandon's last name is pronounced "duh Willduh." The format of the first "d" in documents about him is split pretty much evenly between "de" and "De." His own signature is with a lower-case "d", connecting the "de" with the "Wilde."

All Fall Down
The Brandon deWilde Story

1

A boy who will melt your heart

In the fall of 1948, Brandon deWilde was a second-grader who lived behind a white picket fence on Westminster Road in the Long Island suburb of Baldwin. He struggled with math, played cowboys and Indians in the woods behind his house, and was collecting Corn Flakes box tops for a Space Cadet decoder ring.

Then, as in the story of a mysterious gunfighter and the child who worships him, a stranger appeared and changed the lives of Brandon and his family forever.

Terry Fay was a casting director for the theater producer Robert Whitehead who, with his wife, Virginia Cowen, and Oliver Rea and Stanley Martineau, was producing Carson McCullers's stage treatment of her 1946 novella, *The Member of the Wedding*.

The story revolves around a trio of misfits who cling to each other for comfort. Julie Harris was playing the title character, a tomboy named Frankie Addams, and the legendary Ethel Waters was returning to the Broadway stage as the motherly housekeeper Berenice.

But less than six weeks before the Broadway opening the producers didn't have a John Henry West.

Frankie's cousin, whom she alternately babies and bullies, is introduced in the play as a delicate, active boy, blond and sunburned. Virtually all of the four- to twelve-year-old boys in New York City with actor equity cards had auditioned for the part.

Tommy Rettig was five years away from playing Jeff Miller in the TV show *Lassie* when he was offered the part. But six-year-old Tommy was already tired of the theater. He had toured with Mary Martin for a year in *Annie Get Your Gun* and told the author, "I found it boring doing a play. It must be like doing the same song for years." So he took the movie route, appearing two years later in four of them, including Elia Kazan's *Panic in the Streets*.

In November 1949, the *New York Times* reported that in the producers' continuing quest for a John Henry, Virginia Cowen "will tour the southern states having already been through the east." Both Terry Fay and Carson McCullers peeked into dozens of classrooms, and each producer had ransacked Rolodexes for names of friends with children.

Terry Fay wanted "a darling, nice little boy who doesn't seem too professional." Director Harold Clurman, according to the *New York Times,* wanted "a boy who will melt your heart."

How the Broadway producers and the suburban boy who personified these attributes found each other, Fay related to me forty years later, was "such a funny set of circumstances that it really was kind of kismet.

"I had dropped off a script downtown and ran into someone who was a mutual friend of Fritz's and mine. He said, 'I'm having lunch with Fritz deWilde and you've got to come.' So I did. And I talked to him about coming to read for one of the parts in *The Member of the Wedding* and told him there might be something in it as well for Genie. He said, 'Oh, that'll be terrific.' And then he said, 'I haven't seen you for such a long time and Genie would love to see you. Would you come to dinner one night?'

"I went to his house and there was this marvelous little boy there. I hadn't seen him since he was a baby. He had this slightly husky little voice. Oh, he was just enchanting. And he was seven years old. He was so perfect."

Fay telephoned Fritz, and after reminding him to audition for the part of Frankie's older brother and the groom of the wedding, "I said to him, 'Why don't you bring Brandon? Bring Brandon.'"

Five years later, Brandon's father explained to the *Saturday Evening Post* why he said no. "What scared us the most was that he might turn into a stage brat. I've seen too many of them in my lifetime. A youngster can be ruined when he becomes a professional actor. He starts living in the actor's world — develops a hard-boiled attitude toward everything, worries about billing and reviews and salary. It's terrible. A kid misses out on a normal childhood. Overnight, he goes from ten to 25 — and by the time he's 25, like as not, he's no good as an actor anyway."

Fritz finally gave in to Fay's prodding and he and Brandon went into the city together to read for the director, performing a scene from the play *On Borrowed Time*. "I played Grandpa and Brandon played the kid and Mr. Clurman OK'd him immediately," Fritz deWilde told the *New Yorker*. A reading with Julie Harris was scheduled next.

On a drive to Virginia to his aunt's wedding, Brandon said in the 1962 book, *A Profile of an Art*, "My father and mother taught me the lines of the play. We worked on them carefully and seriously. My father would cue me and I would say the lines, trying to understand them."

Almost forty years later, at a coffee shop on West Forty-Second Street during rehearsals for *Driving Miss Daisy*, Julie Harris recalled the reading with Brandon. "He had a little Buster Brown white shirt and knee socks. He wasn't an actor; he wasn't trained in any way. But he had been taught his few little lines and when he said, 'Frankie, you want me to get the weekend bag?' his little eyes crinkled, he smiled, and he really looked at me and there was something so dear and warm about him."

Brandon said in *The Player* that the decision to become an actor "was pretty much left up to me." Robert Whitehead phoned his parents to tell them he had the part and to get their approval, and then asked to speak to Brandon. "He asked me whether I really wanted to do it, and I just said, 'yes.'"

Another little boy had also been offered the role, with the idea that the two youngsters would divide the eight performances a week. Six-year-old Chris Kirkland was the son of Haila Stoddard, an actress, and Jack Kirkland, a playwright (*Tobacco Road*). Chris is also the stepbrother of the ballerina Gelsey Kirkland. Haila said that Robert Whitehead advised her to "go home and have a big think," about putting her son in the play. Her "no," she said, "was a hangover from my own father who insisted that I finish college before taking up the theater as a career."

In a Whitehead-Rea Productions, Inc., press release, Brandon's parents are quoted as saying, "We thought it over for days. Finally we worked out all the details of a plan we think will let Brandon do this role and still grow up to be a normal boy. Also we had an agreement that Brandon would stay in the play only as long as he is happy and does not become a whining child professional."

The starring role on Broadway that had eluded both Genie and Fritz despite years of training and auditioning had been dropped into their little boy's lap.

Brandon's show-business experience was sitting, according to *Family Circle*, in the peanut gallery of *The Howdy Doody Show* and, according to his best boyhood friend, Maarten Heybroek, in the bleachers for the live taping of the *Morey Amsterdam Show*. He also acted in two school plays. In the first grade, he was one of three silent kittens and tried to sneak off the stage, and in Sunday school his part was announcing, "We have written a play and are now going to do it for you."

Whitehead said the producers detected in Brandon the

"plaintiveness and life-affirming quality" of John Henry. Being blond, he looked the part and being "a squirmy little thing," as described by his second grade teacher Florence Reis, he fit McCullers's description of "active." He sounded right. McCullers's story was set in Georgia, and Brandon had a trace of his mother's southern drawl. And, finally, he could sing.

In the *Saturday Evening Post*, Genie told a reporter that the one extraordinary thing about Brandon was "his feeling about music. He was responsive to songs and could sing a melody in tune when he was only eighteen months old. We still have a tape recording of him singing Jesus Loves Me when he was two years old, and he sang every note of the hymn perfectly." In the second act of *The Member of the Wedding* John Henry nestles with Frankie in Berenice's broad lap and brings down the curtain with a verse from the spiritual song "His Eye is on the Sparrow."

His struggle to read was not a handicap. Ethel Waters proved to be the slowest of the three principals to learn her lines, and according to Lester Polakov, who was in charge of the lighting and set design as well as costumes, when she stumbled over a line, Brandon jumped in with it. "He did it two or three times," said Polakov. "Finally she said, 'Thank you sugar. Apparently you're trying to help me. But I have to get it myself!'"

Julie Harris said that for the first week of rehearsals, Brandon "was just like a little parrot. He just parroted his lines in singsong and you thought, 'Is he ever going to stop doing that? Is what he is saying ever going to mean anything?' Then one night he began to say the lines instead of singing them. And we were all sort of holding our breath, looking at this tiny child really acting. I looked down at his father sitting in the auditorium and Fritz was crying. And I thought, 'Oh God. He's really taking off. He's really doing the part.'

"So that magic happened and we had a beautiful John Henry West."

2

Members of the whole world

Genie (Eugenia) Wilson studied dramatics from the age of twelve in her hometown of Norfolk, Virginia. At eighteen, a southern belle with long, honey-colored hair, she had two walk-on parts in summer stock. The year after that, in 1937, she struck out for New York City with another starry-eyed friend, Margaret Garland. Every day, wearing the jacket and skirt, hat, gloves, and high heels that were the uniform of big-city girls, they made the rounds of Broadway's theatrical offices and scanned the actor equity notices for casting tips. To close the gap between the money from home and sparse modeling and radio work, and the rent on their cramped apartment, they sold makeup at the Arnold Constable department store on Fifth Avenue and Fortieth Street and compared different brands of hand cream for a marketing firm.

Frederic, known to all as Fritz, was an only child. His father, Andre, was an insurance agent and his grandfather immigrated to America from Holland, shortening the family name from Neitzel-deWilde.

At the University of Kentucky, Fritz belonged to the Delta Tau Delta fraternity, an honorary society of theater people called the Strollers, and the exclusive Scabbard and Blade dedicated to "defending military tradition," according to classmate William Dyer. He loved music and played a variety of instruments, occasionally gigging with his saxophone in clubs around Long Island.

Andre hoped Fritz would follow him into the insurance field. Fritz only knew he didn't want to write policies. At the University of Kentucky, he was cast as the comic foil Mercutio in *Romeo and Juliet*, and his life's direction was set. He spent the summer after college acting in a theater company and then moved to New York City.

Fritz and Genie met in 1939 at a large, round table by the basement stairs in Walgreen's drugstore on Forty-Fourth Street. This hangout for unemployed actors was presided over by Henry Moritz. Two years after they arrived in New York City, they got their theatrical break.

Genie's ticket was the part of a child bride, Pearl, in the national touring company of *Tobacco Road*, the longest-running play on Broadway until it was usurped later that year by *Life with Father*.

As reported in the *Norfolk Ledger-Dispatch*, "Opening after only one rehearsal in one's first speaking part in a play and on top of that opening in one's hometown, is an ordeal no budding actress should be forced to face." Genie told the paper that the event was "the most exciting, but frightening" of her—albeit brief—career.

Fritz joined the road company of *Little Foxes* as an assistant stage manager and understudy to Dan Duryea. Tallulah Bankhead was reprising her starring role on Broadway.

Fritz and Genie were married in Reno, which was the first city after their engagement within driving distance of their respective touring companies.

But acting glory for both of them was short-lived. Fritz was a reserve officer. A week into rehearsals for his new play, *Brother Cain*, he was called to active duty, receiving a commission to Fort

Niagara in Youngstown, New York. As for Genie, her sister June Berry said that she "played her last performance in *Tobacco Road* a short time after the marriage because she wanted to be with Fritz from then on."

On April 9, 1942, at St. Mary's Hospital in Brooklyn, their son was born, christened Andre Brandon deWilde. The middle name came from the Brandons of Haddon Hall on Genie's side, one of whom was Sir Charles, who married a sister of King Henry VII.

When the war ended, Fritz found that while his boyish face had worked for him when he was twenty-two because he could play teenagers as well as young men, looking like Huckleberry Finn at twenty-seven locked him out of leading-man roles.

Luckily, the fledging medium of TV was opening up a stream of jobs for out-of-work actors, and Fritz was able to patch together a living. By the time he joined the cast of *The Member of the Wedding*, he was a skit actor on NBC's *Musical Merry Go-Round* and had a respectable list of theatrical credits as supporting actor, understudy, and assistant stage director.

* * *

Carson McCullers was twenty when she set about to write her first book. Her heroine was drawn from her own adolescence. Growing up in the south, she was gawky, romantic, and hypersensitive—a misfit who wanted desperately to belong.

In the five years it took her to finish *The Member of the Wedding*, she had published *The Heart Is a Lonely Hunter* and *Reflections in a Golden Eye*. Now Tennessee Williams proclaimed her America's greatest living writer, and it was he who persuaded McCullers to turn the book into a play.

The Member of the Wedding opens on Frankie's twelfth summer, in a sweltering kitchen where Frankie is playing one of an endless series of card games with her only friends, John Henry and Berenice. Frankie's mother is dead, and her father is as tired and preoccupied as any hardworking widower. Frankie is too old to be John Henry's playmate but also too young to join the girls with figures and long hair who meet in the neighborhood clubhouse.

Berenice is thrice divorced and once widowed. John Henry's mother is always out. "He ate lunch with Frankie, and dinner, and Frankie could not make him go home," McCullers writes.

But Frankie doesn't think of John Henry and Berenice as lonely. Berenice has her clubs, and John Henry, his imaginary friends. "All the other people had a 'we' to claim, all except her," McCullers writes. When word comes that Frankie's brother is getting married, the news falls like a floodlight into her dark world. She imagines the couple will take her with them: "At last she knew just who she was and understood where she was going. She loved her brother and the bride and she was a member of the wedding."

She announces to Berenice and John Henry that when she, her brother, and the bride leave the place where her soldier brother is stationed, "We're going to more places than you ever thought about or even knew existed… strangers will rush to meet us and say: 'Come in! Come in!'…We will be members of the whole world!"

The doors were as closed to Brandon, Julie, and Ethel in 1949 as to the characters they played.

Brandon was a child before the youth culture in America kicked in. Most movies were made for adults—no John Hughes spinning gold from tales of teen angst. The covers of *TIME* displayed ink drawings of the jowly, gray-haired men who ran the country and not girl singers wearing bits of lingerie and lots of tattoos.

Julie Harris was twenty-four. To look half her age as Frankie, her long red hair was lopped off, and almost no makeup crossed her delicate features. She first acted in a high school production of *The Hunchback of Notre Dame* in Grosse Pointe, Michigan, and between 1945 and her casting as Frankie in 1948, she was in eleven Broadway shows. "The only reason I didn't get a bad review was my roles were so insignificant, critics didn't realize I was on stage," she told the author.

Irving Berlin wrote three songs for Ethel Waters, and at one point, she was the highest-paid woman on Broadway. But a series of bad career moves, bad investments, and bad men followed, and when Robert Whitehead went looking for her for the part of Berenice she was in debt and living in a Chicago boarding house.

Deeply religious, she told him, "I don't see no God in Berenice," and agreed to play the part only when he softened the character and allowed her to sing a signature gospel song, "His Eye is on the Sparrow." That Waters originally rejected the part, poor as she was, typified the setbacks that Whitehead and his company suffered all the way up to opening curtain.

No playwright the producers approached thought drama could be spun from the dreams and disappointments of a black maid and a girl in love with a wedding so McCullers wrote the script herself. Cheryl Crawford, a giant in the theater who cofounded both the Actor's Studio and the Group Theater, advised her to toss it in the trash.

In the best of times on Broadway, it would be tricky to mine box office gold from McCullers's ethereal script, but the late 1940s were Broadway's worst yet. In 1949, there were sixty-two Broadway shows, down from 268 in 1927.

The reason could be found in Norman Rockwell's November, 1949, *Saturday Evening Post* cover in which an excited homeowner is leaning out of his window to look up at a man installing the television antenna on his roof that rises higher than a church steeple. Hundreds of thousands of New Yorkers now had a TV set. If they had a hankering for live theater, there were a dozen televised choices every week, under titles like "Mystery Theater", and "Actor's Studio." Without leaving their living rooms, they could also laugh with the Goldbergs, discover a star on "Arthur Godfrey's Talent Scouts," or root for their local football team or favorite Roller Derby star. On Saturday nights starting in February 1950, the country was riveted by the hijinks of Sid Caesar and friends on the trailblazing TV variety series "Your Show of Shows." Caesar related in his autobiography how a delegation of Broadway producers visited NBC-TV studios and begged them to switch the airdate to a weekday.

TV wasn't Broadway's only problem. John Chapman, in *The Burns Mantle Best Plays of 1949-1950*, cited skyrocketing production and maintenance costs for the challenging times on Broadway. He added, "It often seemed to me that the public wanted to see only one show, *South Pacific* [which opened in April of 1949], and it went grudgingly to something else because tickets to this astonishing box-office freak were not available."

The setbacks only invigorated Robert Whitehead, described by Arthur Miller as "one of a handful of producers who longed for artistically ambitious and socially interesting plays and could put their money where their mouth was."

"I become involved in a project when no one else will touch it," Whitehead said in between productions of *Medea* with Judith Anderson and *Crime and Punishment* with John Gielgud.

According to a contemporary news account about *The Member of the Wedding*, "The Broadway big-wigs just didn't think the drama would be a commercial success. But Whitehead and Rea were determined and they alerted friends that small investments, even as low as $50, would be gratefully accepted. Terry Fay tapped friends and relatives (25 of them) and managed to amass $2,500 on her own. Others around town who believed in the play and knew of *Wedding*'s financial difficulties did the same."

Lester Polakov said, "We had to account for every pair of socks, but we scrimped through."

Harold Clurman was a cofounder of New York City's Group Theater and veteran of forty plays including *All My Sons* but he had to summon all his resources to direct this cast. Ethel Waters was an earthy, street-wise woman who disdained formal training, and Julie Harris was a college graduate and method actress. Polakov recalled Julie mentioning the method catchphrase "effective memory" at one rehearsal. "Ethel said, 'I don't give a damn about all that. I've lived, had my personal experiences, my sorrows. No one has to tell me I have to learn any method to act.' Everyone looked at each other—she was a method actress from way back. She was *the* method actor."

Polakov said that with Brandon, "We were stumped. Because not only had Brandon never been onstage, he didn't even know that stages existed. He had never been in a theater." He said that when Brandon saw the curtain come down at the first dress rehearsal he yelled, "Look at the wall coming down. It's falling! It's falling!"

In mid-December Brandon rode the train to Philadelphia with his family for the traditional week of out-of-town tryouts, where kinks were worked out of Broadway-bound plays before they were unveiled to the all-powerful New York City theater critics.

Genie and Fritz had numerous footholds in the play. Fritz was the acting coach for both Brandon and Brandon's understudy Robert Mariotti, whose parents were both deaf-mutes. Fritz also played a customer in the bar scene. Genie failed to get the part of John Henry's mother because she looked too young but was cast as understudy for the bride.

The Member of the Wedding previewed in Philadelphia on December 22, 1949, at the Walnut Street Theater. There were paying audience members for the first time, and a row of critics stared ahead, notepads on their laps. "Nobody had much hope for it," one of them, John Chapman, wrote in the Burns-Mantle book about the theatrical season.

Variety reported that Brandon "had stage fright so badly just before the play's premiere there was a several-moments question whether the opening curtain would have to be held. During rehearsals the youngster had been told about playing to an audience and waiting for laughs but when he heard the overture and the conversational hum out front just before the performance was to start he became panicky. Despite reassurances from the show's leads and from the stage manager Jus Addiss young deWilde said he'd forgotten his lines and begged not to have the curtain raised. However after being comforted by his actor parents he dried his eyes and agreed to go on. After getting a hand on his first exit the kid was completely composed and, according to other cast members, was the only one to give a letter-perfect performance."

This is how Julie Harris remembers it: "We were all assembled on stage—'places please!'—and we heard the suppressed roar of the audience from behind the curtain. Brandon looked astonished and then troubled as it dawned on him that all those people would be watching the play, and the tears started falling down his cheeks. Fritz walked on stage from the wings to comfort him. Ethel put her arms around him. We all said it would be OK. Then, the curtain rose and there he was again—John Henry in his cousin Frankie's garden, welcoming the bride- and groom-to-be. He was adorable—bright, spontaneous, charming—and won the audience completely."

And here's Brandon's account to columnist Sidney Fields: "The stage looked like the biggest place in the world. Everyone and everything on it looked big except me. I hadn't known there would be an orchestra and the unexpectedness of it frightened me. My father told me, 'you're the only one who has nothing to worry about because you know your lines.' He wiped my eyes and when I got out there I knew every bit of them."

Fritz's opening-night gift to Brandon was two railroad switches for an electric train set in the deWildes' basement. ("The most magnificent train set I had ever seen," said family friend Lou Peterson.)

Another gift to Brandon was this review by Henry T. Murdock of the *Philadelphia Inquirer*: "He is one of rarities in the theater, a child player who seems to know what he is doing all the time without doing it precociously."

Murdock summed up the qualified praise for the play itself: "It could very likely be that play you wait for all season, the one play that suddenly lights up the theater with a dramatic impact that makes the previous offerings, no matter how well written and acted, seem on the frail side. May be, we say, for this play is deadline-defying. It is long and its physical maneuvering is clumsy."

There were two sets: Frankie's kitchen and the Blue Moon Café where Frankie has a disastrous encounter with a soldier after she runs away from home. According to Polakov, "Someone said it might be better staying in one place and suggested taking out the two scenes at the café. There were discussions and arguments, and we decided to try it. The new version debuted at a matinee, and at the end of it we were all very excited, because suddenly it worked."

Of the five small roles jettisoned, one was Fritz's. But Robert Whitehead needed Fritz in the company to make sure that Brandon behaved so he made him understudy to the groom and assistant to the stage manager.

The New York City opening was at the Empire Theater on Forty-Sixth Street and Broadway on January 5, 1950. The rococo hall was electric with excitement because of the positive reports that had filtered back from Philadelphia.

Backstage, wearing only a faded, powder-blue sunsuit, gold-rimmed eyeglasses without the lenses, and a little tin donkey on a cord around his neck, Brandon riffled through a stack of telegrams on his dressing room table, including one from his teacher. "What are these, bills?" he asked his mother. The makeup artist popped in to run a brown pencil over his pale eyebrows and smudge some rouge on his cheeks and lips.

"There was a question of would he remember his lines, and there was someone at the side-stage ready to cue him, and he amazed everybody," said Polakov. Ethel Waters, too, who during the play's run in Philadelphia still struggled with her lines, was letter perfect on the first night that really counted.

The angel wings that Brandon wears on one of his dress-up forays in the play prefigured the tragedy that opens the third act: John Henry, whose earlier complaints about not feeling well were discounted by Berenice, is dead. Frankie, suddenly a young lady, is preoccupied with her new best friend. Berenice has given Frankie's father notice that she is quitting and doesn't expect Frankie to visit: "Your road is already strange to me," Berenice tells Frankie. Berenice is left alone in the kitchen. She picks up the doll that Janice gave Frankie and Frankie in turn gave John Henry and hums the first lines of "*His Eye Is on the Sparrow.*"

As the opening night curtain came down, the crowd leapt to their feet and brought out Julie, Ethel, and Brandon for a half dozen curtain calls. Julie ran offstage and collapsed.

Polakov said that he looked up at Carson McCullers in her box seat and "Her face was bathed in tears."

"Out of nothing but air and genius, an affecting play was made," wrote Brooks Atkinson, chief theater critic for the *New York Times*. Whitehead told the author, "the conditions just fell into place, and it was a beautiful, moving, and poetic piece."

The three stars stayed behind to pose for publicity photos, possibly by Richard Avedon, since he was the production's photographer. Jus Addiss was leaving after midnight when he saw a throng of autograph seekers at the stage door and at the cynosure, Brandon painstakingly printing onto a theater program a name that a fan was spelling out.

Haila Stoddard said the morning of the opening, "Chris came up to me and said, 'I'd like to send a telegram to my friends because they were so nice to me.'" The following morning, he brought her the *New York Times'* theater section, the front emblazoned with a photo of *The Member of the Wedding.* "He said, 'You know, Mom, the play is a hit. That doesn't happen very often.'" Chris Kirkland later said that he kept track of Brandon's career from that moment on because "there for the grace of a more pushy stage mother went I."

Howard Barnes of the *New York Herald Tribune* remarked

on Brandon's "perfect timing" and "exceptional skill." Brooks Atkinson wrote, "Everyone is in love with Brandon deWilde's sober and plump little performance as the boy next door."

Said Genie, "In our home we had nurtured the one form of theatrical life we had always disapproved—a child actor—and we were stuck with him."

3

Golden boy

Lester Polakov painted a portrait of Brandon on a swing suspended by balloons, high above Manhattan. Genie told a newspaper that this painting, which hung in the family living room, was "reminiscent of the collective deWilde state of mind at the time."

The day after the play opened on Broadway, according to Florence Reis, "The children came in in the morning and said, 'Brandon's not here. Isn't he coming?' and I just said 'no.' I didn't say why." Only she and little Maarten Heybroek knew that he had come home after midnight, the toast of Broadway. Brandon showed up at class in the afternoon, and when he returned home, four reporters were on his front step.

On Sunday, his face was on the cover of the Long Island magazine, *Newsday*. Three weeks later he was featured in a four-page spread on the play in *LIFE*. One of the photos showed him sashaying across the room in Berenice's high heels, hat, and purse. Forty years later, a school friend told me, "I remember that silly picture. It certainly didn't help his standing in the neighborhood."

Almost immediately there was a six-month wait for tickets

at the box office. Reis saw the play with a group of faculty members and remembered thunderous ovations for Ethel, Julie, and Brandon. She said John Henry was "typical of the little Brandon I had in school, except he had these huge glasses." Brandon's fourth-grade teacher, Helene Light, remembered that on the way home, "He was on the same train as us. He was so happy about that. He kept turning around and shouting, 'my teachers are on this train!'"

Mary Martin and Humphrey Bogart were two of the scores of celebrities who paid backstage visits. Betty Lou Holland, who played Frankie in the road show, said Humphrey Bogart "just loved the play" and related to her that Brandon, evidently forgetting he was wearing prop glasses, once put his finger through the frames to scratch his eye.

Brandon's free moments were monopolized by the press. "What's cooking? Fried hot dogs!" is how he greeted a *New Yorker* reporter, according to that magazine's January 28, 1950 "Talk of the Town."

His trademark was curtain-straight, white-blond hair, and it was a rare reporter who didn't use the word "towheaded" to describe him. Reporters also glommed onto his slightly bucked, gap-toothed grin. Reis said this last feature wasn't unusual to her: "I used to tell my second-graders, 'You know why you're my favorite class? You all have big smiles with an empty space.'"

Whitehead theorized that the play struck a chord with audiences because the unlikely friendship of Frankie, Berenice, and John Henry proved there was hope for peace, a welcome message five years after the war. An essay by Brooks Atkinson in the *New York Times* echoed this: "Nothing of great importance happens; some of the peripheral things that do happen have no pertinent relation to the play. Neither are there any memorable lines in the dialogue. As a play it is elusive and intangible. But it gives a vivid impression of life being lived with concentrated vitality by people of force and passion. Although the life it chronicles is commonplace, the people who live it are free individuals who cannot be reduced by circumstances to commonplace levels... It is a poem about the private hope and pain of living at high tension in a heedless world."

Whatever the reasons, Brandon found himself in one of only a handful of bona-fide hits in a theatrical season that offered the only Broadway performance by Grace Kelly (in Strindberg's *The Father*); Shirley Booth's classic and heartrending portrayal of an alcoholic's wife in *Come Back Little Sheba* by the new playwright William Inge; Carol Channing's ticket to iconic status, *Gentleman Prefer Blondes;* and star vehicles for Helen Hayes, Lunt and Fontanne, Katherine Cornell, and Katharine Hepburn.

Robert Mariotti was originally scheduled to play John Henry in the matinee performances of *The Member of the Wedding* but because so many theatergoers inquired specifically about Brandon at the box office, Brandon ended up in all eight weekly performances.

So that Brandon could sleep in after performance nights Genie arranged with the school for Brandon to not come in until 1:00 p.m. Instead, he worked with a private tutor in the morning for an hour and a half. He did his homework on the late afternoon train into the city, and John Henry's death was pushed ahead a few minutes each evening so the boy who played him could ride the 11:00 p.m. train with his parents back into Baldwin.

Six days before Brandon turned eight, he played in both the Saturday matinee and evening performances. Here is what else he did that day: took a morning train into the city and rolled Easter eggs in Central Park, went over some acting notes with Harold Clurman, was surprised with a birthday party in Julie's dressing room, and spent a few hours at CBS studios for a live broadcast of part of the play, to coincide with the upcoming New York Drama Critics Circle Award Show, which awarded *The Member of the Wedding* Best American Play in the 1949-1950 season.

Radio, TV, and movie scripts were tossed Brandon's way like

fistfuls of confetti. He co-starred with Walter Pidgeon on a live radio production of *Fallen Idol*. For the *Philco Television Playhouse*, he co-starred with his father and Rod Steiger in a play written especially for the deWildes called "No Medals on Pop" and with Buster Crabbe in "A Cowboy for Chris." He also played Oliver Twist in a radio broadcast.

The Donaldson Awards, sponsored by Billboard Magazine, were the precursor to the Tony Awards. In the 1949-1950 season, Brandon was the youngest person to ever win one, for best debut performance by a male.

Years after the run of *The Member of the Wedding*, Robert Whitehead said about his leads, "You couldn't find three more completely different people. But when the lights dimmed in the theater, and the curtain rose, there was a life between them that was extraordinary."

So it was off the stage as well. Growing up, Julie's parents played Ethel Waters's blues recordings from the 1920s, and Julie was in the audience when Waters electrified Broadway with her dramatic acting debut in *Mamba's Daughters*. "So I grew up adoring her," she said.

"And Brandon, of course, was a very special child. We just loved each other and took care of each other and enjoyed being with each other. And we trusted each other. Ethel was not...It was not easy for her to trust. But I think she trusted the two of us. She loved Brandon. She called him her Candy.

"I think we instantly felt something for each other. It was very remarkable. We were different ages. Ethel was in her mid-forties, I was twenty-four, and Brandon was seven. Miss Waters, Brandon, and I became one person—all of us in the play did, really."

Harris remembered a postcard she received from Brandon during the play's summer hiatus that referred to their barefoot state on stage. "Dear Julie. My feet have been clean all week. How are yours? Love Brandon."

A year into the play's run Louis Shaeffer wrote in the

Brooklyn Eagle, "A good share of the credit belongs to Ethel Waters, Julie Harris and a wise, bespectacled trouper named Brandon deWilde, who's all of eight years old. After nearly a year of bringing to life an exacting, sensitive script, there isn't a bit of letdown in their playing. Individually, the three are just about perfect in their roles and together they blend with artful harmony in the brilliantly orchestrated performance staged by Harold Clurman. If anything, their performances are deeper, truer and finer than they were on opening night and they were very fine then.

"Confidentially—and I hope this doesn't sound patronizing or smug—I'm very pleased with the theater-going public for making a substantial hit of an 'off-center,' supposedly non-commercial piece like *The Member of the Wedding*. I feel this way because every year there are plays [probably alluding to *Come Back Little Sheba*] which Broadway recognizes as 'artistic successes' but which fail to ingratiate themselves with the public."

Brooks Atkinson's enthusiastic first impression of both the play and Brandon had also strengthened. "In other hands than those of Master deWilde the role could be unbearably precocious. But he plays it with an air of personal indomitability that preserves the independence of the characters amid the whirl of the play. Since he is a good actor with an instinct for making even a small gesture count for something in a performance, Master deWilde could do quite a lot of scene-stealing if he wanted to. Small as he is, he has the magnetic personality of a real performer."

Fritz's cousin Audrey deWilde said that Brandon "was just a natural. He could fall into a part like he was changing clothes. Backstage, Brandon would be talking to his father about his homework right up to the curtain. Then he would just be the part."

One tender scene between Berenice and Frankie had Brandon off to the side, sitting cross-legged on the floor in a tutu.

Lester Polakov was watching the performance from backstage one night when "the audience laughed when it had no business laughing." He looked up at Julie, and then at Ethel, but nothing seemed out of order. Then the next night, at the same moment, there was an even louder laugh. Polakov said the mystery was solved when Ethel stormed off the stage after the scene, muttering, "That child has got to be told some things."

Brandon's costume came out in little points at the bustline, and bored and thinking he wasn't being watched, he had taken hold of the points and pulled them out. Getting a laugh, he did it the second night too. On the third night he repeated the piece of business over and over again but got no laugh. "It was too much," explained Polakov. "He learned how to milk a laugh and how not to milk a laugh."

"Coughing," Julie Harris said with a mischievous grin when asked about Brandon's scene stealing. "When he'd get a cold, he'd cough a lot. A little boy, sitting on the floor in his bare feet coughing, and the audience wouldn't listen to what anybody else was saying. I remember saying to him (whispering loudly) 'Brandon! You've got to try not to cough while we're talking.' He did try—cough, cough."

Harris shook her head and laughed. "Children and animals. Never act with children and animals. But he was terrific. He just strutted around and enjoyed himself, which is what he should have been doing."

He was also an adept ad-libber. Julie Harris swung a doll in one scene, and during one performance she swung too hard and was left holding an unattached arm. "Pause of a few seconds," she recalled, "and then he said, 'Frankie, I think this doll needs a doctor.'

"Once, the curtain didn't come down at the end of the first act. Brandon and I were on stage and I had finished speaking—and no curtain. So I turned and whispered, 'Come on Brandon,' and we ran off-stage. He turned to me and said, 'Julie, you called me Brandon instead of John Henry!'"

Lou Peterson, writer of a groundbreaking play in the 1950s about a young black man growing up in a middle-class neighborhood, was an understudy and assistant stage manager in *The Member of the Wedding* and Brandon's tutor on the road. He said, "We did have a wonderful time in that company. It was like an enlarged family because there was a child on board, and everybody loved Brandon. He was probably the most adored child of anybody in the theater I've ever known."

* * *

The May 1954 *Saturday Evening Post* observed that most child actors "are coy, artificial, repressed children, articulating in British accents as if mechanically echoing their dramatic coaches. They make the rounds of the auditions and the readings and the rehearsals, eternally accompanied by the mother who patiently waits for hours, either knitting or doing crossword puzzles or reading paper-backed reprints. Sometimes these children are from poor families and the jobs they pick up in television are a very crucial help in keeping a family afloat financially."

However, "some of them are healthy, reasonable, rambunctious, normal children, like Brandon."

With the excitement that descended upon the seven-year-old, only a certain fanaticism on the part of Brandon's parents could ensure that these adjectives continued to pertain to him. Robert Whitehead said, "It wasn't so easy for Brandon's parents to give him a normal upbringing after the play became a success, but they did their best."

At the parent-teacher conference before Brandon was cast in the role of John Henry, Genie asked Florence Reis how she could bring up his grade in math, telling her, "I can take a B, but C's bother me." Reis said that after he got the role, that concern shifted. "She wanted to make sure he had a normal life. I used to feel so worried for her because she was so concerned about him."

The attempts to keep him down to earth were trumpeted in the press with headlines like: "The deWildes' Formula for Prodigy: Real Boy 1st, Child Star 2nd" and "Rich Actor, 8, Empties Garbage."

When he was eighteen, Brandon told a reporter, "I'm only now beginning to understand what went on back then. My parents didn't show me any reviews or let me see any awards. I think they tried to keep me from getting conceited." Fritz and Genie told Brandon that the applause and acclaim were for the character he was playing, not for him personally. They also vowed to keep him out of private performing arts schools. "We don't want him hearing the talk of precocious stage children about the parts they've played and the salaries they've earned," Fritz told a reporter.

A fine line was walked between nurturing him as a performer and keeping him a child. According to the January 9, 1951, *New York Post*, twice a week, one or both of Brandon's parents sat in the audience of *The Member of the Wedding*. They made sure that his performance stayed fresh and that he didn't add "business" or dialogue. If the performance was all right, they said nothing.

Their efforts were echoed in the community.

During Brandon's seven years at Lenox Elementary School he starred in two hit Broadway plays, what some consider the greatest Western movie ever made, and his own TV show — yet the school granted him a skimpy page and a half in its commemorative scrapbook.

In the scrapbook, under a headline "Some of Lenox school pupils become famous" is a newspaper clip from the *Baldwin Citizen* announcing the casting of Brandon on Broadway. It shares the page with notices of Greg Murphy appearing on the TV show *Small Fry*, "as one of a group of 10 selected in response to a letter he wrote telling of his part in selling flowers for the polio drive," and Derek Ter Haar and Richard Thorns appearing on WNBC's *Quiz Kids*.

Florence Reis said, "We all went along our same ways and

treated him like all the children in our other classes, and didn't put him on a pedestal." She said the press only intruded in her classroom once. "The mother didn't want reporters coming to the school, and the principal, who was a very proper English woman, probably wouldn't have allowed it."

Kenneth Schmidt, a classmate of Brandon's through *The Member of the Wedding, Shane* and *Goodbye My Lady,* said, "I never really thought of him as being in the movie business."

Greg Murphy recalled seeing "a couple of awards and plaques" in Brandon's house but said they were "more flotsam and jetsam accumulated over the years, rather than being formally displayed." Rick Williams, who met Brandon in the Boy Scouts when they were ten-years-old in 1952, said that Brandon's parents were "probably the way all of ours were back then. The mother was one of the nicest people you could find. The father was a little remote. He was a nice person but a little hurried and temperamental—caught up with his career. Brandon was in the same trouble as I was. Report card time we were grounded." Maarten Heybroek's family left Baldwin when he was in the sixth grade, but he said that up until then, as far as possessions went, Brandon's "wish list was as long as mine."

William Morris agent Ed Robbins represented Sal Mineo before he teamed up with James Dean in *East of Eden* and Patty Duke in 1959 when she was thirteen and mesmerizing Broadway as Helen Keller in *The Miracle Worker*. Robbins started working with Brandon when Brandon was twenty-one.

The life of a young actor, he told the author, "is so far afield from what we would consider a normal upbringing. There, you go to school, play, have dinner, maybe on the weekend go to a movie. Here you have a young person who'd be involved in a very emotional relationship on stage. Suddenly, the curtain comes down at an hour when most children certainly are in bed; he hears applause and takes a curtain call. It's not what the majority of children face, and it's got to affect them somehow.

"How does a child separate fantasy from reality? We like to

think it's easy for an older person, say, starting out at twenty-one to do this, but what goes on in the mind of a six-year-old?"

He was "very taken" with the deWildes. "There was nothing show-bizzy about them. They seemed like a lovely couple who were very proud of their son and just wanted the best for him. They were trying to give him the best of both worlds—the opportunity of being an actor but a home life as well to maintain a set of values. His parents always wanted Brandon to retain his sense of the world away from the world of acting."

Martha Carson, a long-time family friend, said that Genie "was not the typical stage mother. She was always very cautious and careful about the projects he worked on, making sure he didn't get into sleazy company. [The deWildes] were always surrounded by nice people who had good reputations in the business."

John Anderson had a similar career to Fritz. He amassed a slew of acting and understudying roles on stage as early as 1937 and then became a stage manager, assisting Fritz and working on his own in shows such as the original Broadway run of *Camelot*. He told me, "Brandon was very lucky to have them as parents, though not lucky in the long run."

His parents' efforts to keep Brandon normal outside of the theater also made him a better actor inside it. The movie executive who nurtured the career of Shirley Temple was Winfield Sheehan. In Temple's autobiography *Child Star*, she said that Sheehan "was very anxious I shouldn't become spoiled because if I started admiring myself it would be sure to come out on the screen" and the very quality that made her special would be gone.

Ed Robbins saw Brandon in *The Member of the Wedding* and said that what set him apart from other child actors was that he "seemed very real. What you saw was in a way what the person really was."

Brandon made two hundred dollars a week for *The Member of the Wedding*, a little more than twice the minimum pay set by the actors' union. Every TV spot netted him $147.50. All of this was funneled into a trust fund that, by 1954, was estimated to be worth a quarter of a million dollars. According to the *Saturday Evening Post*, the deWilde home at this time was valued at $16,000.

Brandon's trust fund had stipulations that became a model for protecting a child actor's earnings. Brandon was named a ward of court, and money could only be withdrawn from his account with a formal petition and the bank president's signature.

His weekly allowance, for jawbreakers and Gene Autry comic books at the Main Street candy store and root beer floats at Baldwin Drugs, was the going rate at school—ten cents at the start of the play's run and fifty cents by mid-1952 when it ended. For this, he had to bring in the garbage can, set the table, dry the dishes, and be a good boy in the theater and out of it.

But Brandon's new world couldn't help but seep into his old one. Florence Reis said that when her class put on a play, "We were all ready to start and he said to me in a loud whisper, 'Mrs. Reis! Douse the house lights!' (I decided he wouldn't have a big part because the children would resent him even more. So I gave him a very minor role. I didn't even tell the mother why. I hope she understood.)"

Jimmy Lydon was the title character in the early 1940s movies *Tom Brown School Days* and *Henry Aldrich*. When he was a fourteen-year-old on tour with a theater company, his chaperone, to be sure that his charge would be onstage when the curtain rose, locked him in his hotel room alone every morning until curtain call.

Brandon was at the opposite end of the spectrum of this road experience with the year-long tour of *The Member of the Wedding*, which began in the spring of 1951. Fritz had to stay behind to coach the boy taking over Brandon's part in New York City, but every free afternoon, mother and son would visit the towns' museums, zoos, parks, or libraries. Cast members got together most Sundays.

Reis said, "Genie was determined, 'this is going to be a normal child.'" And the parents' diligence seemed to be paying off. "I had Brandon before he became famous and after he became famous," she said "and personally, I didn't see any difference."

* * *

Between the play's opening and its first anniversary, America was transformed: 1949 was a year of forced gaiety, trying to resume life under the threat of the mushroom cloud detonated over Hiroshima just four years earlier. America's sex goddess Rita Hayworth married the Aga Kahn, and a last-game home run by Joe DiMaggio gave Casey Stengel's New York Yankees a World Series win over the Dodgers.

A few months into 1950, a senator waved a stack of papers, saying they contained the names of 205 communists in the state department, and McCarthyism was born. In late June, the communist North Korean army smashed across the thirty-eighth parallel into South Korea. The spirit of the country grew darker as the year progressed.

Film director Fred Zinnemann asked his New York City agent to send him the script of *The Member of the Wedding* after he watched it on Broadway. The agent attached a note dated December 5, 1950, that reflected the mood back east: "These have been two tragic weeks in New York. The accident with the Long Island railroad in which so many lives were lost, mile-a-minute gales, and now the realization that the boys won't be home for Christmas."

In the new year, flashbulbs and large crowds greeted the Hollywood unveiling of a bomb shelter. Around the same time, Brooks Atkinson wrote, "While the rest of us have been going about our affairs and altering our moods to conform with external circumstances, *The Member of the Wedding* has remained constant and intact at the Empire Theater. To revisit the play is to catch a rueful glimpse of the old America when external affairs seemed less urgent than the torment and turbulence of a graceless adolescent girl in Georgia."

The Member of the Wedding closed on Broadway on March 17, 1951, after 492 performances. Brandon had not missed one.

Julie remembered when the curtain came down for the last time.

"They came to take Brandon's props— his little, tiny glasses and the tin donkey he wore around his neck. The property man came to take those back, and he said, 'I don't want to. *Sob, sob.* I want to keep those so I can remember it.' "And Ethel said, 'You can keep them, sugar. You can keep them, my baby.' I remember him sitting on her lap. It was spring outside, Brandon crying, and Ethel comforting him and saying, 'You can keep those glasses.'"

Julie, Ethel, and Brandon were all somebodies now.

Julie began rehearsals for *I am a Camera*, with Terry Fay's sister Patricia taking over the role of Frankie on a new road tour. The Christopher Isherwood play was the darling of the 1951 season, winning the New York Drama Critics Circle Award and making Julie a full-fledged star. After a fifty-year career that paired her with James Dean in *East of Eden* and Rod Steiger in *Requiem for a Heavyweight*, she would say about *The Member of the Wedding*, "I never had another experience like that. Nobody's ever written like Carson McCullers, and I don't look for it to ever happen again."

In the fall of 1950, Ethel was filming episodes of the hit sitcom *Beulah*, playing the character of the warm-hearted maid who was originally on radio's *Fibber McGee and Molly*. She left the show after two years, complaining it was derogatory to her race, and the role was taken over by *Gone with the Wind's* Hattie McDaniel. For years after that, Waters toured with *The Member of the Wedding*.

Brandon would soon reunite with Julie and Ethel for the filming of the movie version of their play. And his summer was spent on an outdoor movie set in Wyoming with the premier director in Hollywood. George Stevens had just wrapped *A Place in the Sun* with Elizabeth Taylor and Montgomery Clift when he caught Brandon in "No Medals on Pop," just as he was mulling over who could play the boy who idolizes a gunfighter named Shane.

Three other children were up for this role. Bobby Driscoll, the first actor placed under contract with Walt Disney, had starred in *Song of the South* and *Treasure Island* and won an Academy Award for Outstanding Juvenile Actor in 1949. Fifteen-year-old Dean Stockwell had acted with Frank Sinatra, Errol Flynn, and Lionel Barrymore and starred in *The Boy with Green Hair*. The third contender was David John Stollery, who was a year older than Brandon and, notwithstanding his film debut at six with Bing Crosby (in *A Connecticut Yankee in King Arthur's Court*) and appearance on stage in Robert Whitehead's *Medea*, had the slimmest resume.

The three veered in vastly different directions after *Shane*. Dean Stockwell kept acting in high-caliber productions, including a spate of art movies for Wim Wenders and David Lynch in the 1980s, and was nominated for an Academy Award at the age of fifty-two. David Stollery was named Child Actor of the Year in 1954 for his role in the Broadway revival of *On Borrowed Time* and peaked in popularity two years later with a starring role in the *Mickey Mouse Club* TV serial *Spin and Marty*. He left acting for college and became one of the top car designers in the country. Bobby Driscoll was perhaps the most envied child of them all because of his long association with Walt Disney, and he had the greatest fall. A few short years after he was the voice of Disney's Peter Pan his career was relegated to parts in TV anthologies. By the age of twenty-five there were no jobs at all, and he was quoted as saying, "I have found that memories are not very useful. I was carried on a silver platter...and then dumped in the garbage." He died broke at thirty-one in 1968 from an apparent drug overdose.

But in 1950, each was flying high. After it was announced

that Brandon would star opposite Jean Arthur and Alan Ladd, one theater critic wrote, "Obviously young Brandon deWilde is going places. And his fine performance in *The Member of the Wedding* is only the first act."

4

Going places

Shane opens with a close-up of Brandon, his slightly crossed, dark blue eyes opening wide as his character spots a stranger riding on horseback into his family's valley.

Brandon's parents turned down twenty-five movie scripts before saying yes to this one. George Stevens chose to direct his first Western after receiving a package that included the 1949 novel by Jack Schaefer, two screen treatments, and this newspaper blurb: "Although not another *Virginian*, it has the same quality, dignity, appeal which made Owen Wisters' previous novel of years ago read by people who scoffed at westerns. A tragic, taut little tale of a grim, unforgettable, mysterious and at times sinister figure of a man."

Shane was the second in Stevens's epic trilogy of American history as seen through the eyes of simple folks who unknowingly created it, dealing with the changeover in the west, from open ranges to fenced-in lots. *A Place in the Sun* examines the shift to urban living: the movie *Giant*, the replacement of oil over cattle as the main source of wealth in the west.

In Schaefer's book, the story unfolds through the eyes of a little boy named Bobby Starrett, and the scriptwriter A.B.

Guthrie kept the boy as the focus, changing his name to Joey.

The title character in *Shane*, who attaches himself to a settler family of husband, wife, and young boy in 1880s Wyoming, is soft-spoken and seems to be as peace-loving as they are. But he is a gunfighter grown tired of killing, determined to put away his guns forever.

There is a showdown between the squatters, families who've fenced in their plots of land, and the cattlemen who want open fields for grazing and water access. Shane straps on his guns and kills again, saving the family he has grown to love but dooming himself.

Both treatments of *Shane* originally presented to Stevens were written with Alan Ladd in mind as the lead. The Foreign Press Association had just named Ladd and Esther Williams the most popular Hollywood stars in the world and he had been Paramount's biggest box-office star for a decade.

Before coming back around to Ladd, George Stevens considered most of the leading men in Hollywood. The finalists to play the troika of Shane and Mr. and Mrs. Starrett were Humphrey Bogart, with Ralph Bellamy, and Anne Baxter; Monty Clift, with Broderick Crawford, and Joan Crawford; and Kirk Douglas in the title role supported by Brian Donleavy and Bette Davis.

Stevens ended up pairing Ladd with Jean Arthur and adding an actor named William Holden, who had a joint contract with Paramount and Columbia. This would have been Holden's twelfth movie in three years, but he was replaced with Van Heflin after griping to the media that he was being overworked. Arthur reached her career peak in the 1930s as a madcap comedienne, receiving her only Oscar nomination for Stevens's *The More the Merrier*.

With Ladd, Stevens's reputation for casting against type was upheld: a five-foot-five slight man with blond hair, whom pulp writer Raymond Chandler tagged as "a boy's idea of a tough guy," would play Schaefer's dark, craggy-faced gunman.

Ladd had shot to fame playing a stoic killer named Philip Raven in the 1942 film noir *This Gun for Hire*. Cynical, sexy, self-contained, his Raven was a different sort of gangster from the Chicago mobster usually portrayed by Hollywood. Richard Schickel called him a killer who "succeeded in reducing murder to an act as irrelevant as crossing the street," but at the same time there was a despair in him that foreshadowed James Dean.

Over the next decade, Ladd played Raven in a string of movie clones. Darryl Zanuck called him "the indestructible man. He stays on top in mediocre films. Imagine where he would be if he were cast in worthwhile and important ones." Alan Ladd was tired of the tough-guy stereotype, too, and wanted to discover how far he could go with better roles.

Lucy Kroll negotiated billing for Brandon that gave him his own frame in the opening credits with the phrase, "Introducing Brandon deWilde." If a movie of his came out before *Shane*, he would get first featured billing. His fifteen-hundred-dollars-a-week salary was a fraction of Alan Ladd's one hundred sixty-three thousand dollars but a fair-sized raise from the four hundred dollars a week he made for the movie version of *The Member of the Wedding*. Fritz was signed as Brandon's acting coach at three hundred fifty dollars a week. Brandon's contract called for an option of a picture a year for two years with a salary rise to two thousand dollars a week, with Fritz getting a hundred-dollar-a-week raise as well. Brandon would also get script approval for his next two movies.

Brandon and his mother flew west on July 15 for nine days of preproduction at the studio, landing in the Hollywood of Frank Sinatra courting Ava, Judy Garland still reigning over MGM, and Liz Taylor in between marriages to Nicky Hilton and Michael Wilding.

Stevens's passion for authenticity was legendary. According to the August 8, 1953, *Saturday Evening Post*, to make sure the actors in the bathing-suit factory in *A Place in the Sun* looked right, he reproduced an assembly line at the studio and put the extras in the picture and Shelley Winters and Montgomery Clift to work for days packaging swimsuits so that when they did it before the camera it was as if they'd been doing it for months.

He naturally shunned the film studio and movie ranch Corriganville that was the outdoor set for hundreds of Westerns, including *The Lone Ranger* TV show, and Brandon spent his ninth summer at the landmark Wort Hotel in Jackson Hole, filming beneath the Grand Tetons. The movie set was a meticulous recreation of a community settled by hardscrabble folk who brought little out with them and had no way to replace what wore out.

The cabins were built to specifications gleaned from paintings by the western artist Charles Russell. Skinnier cows were railed in from the east, and a stream was diverted so that it could flow by the Starrett home.

George Stevens's mania for authenticity was responsible for one of the most compelling aspects of Brandon's character—his patched, ragged, and dirt-encrusted clothes, including overalls that were way too short and as baggy as a burlap sack. "All you have shown is generally good," Stevens wrote to the costume director Joe de Young a week into production. "But I become disturbed when you tell the cameraman that you are using this material because it will give light or bulk. We want these people to wear the things that would have been available to them and that they would wear when they lived in the country at that time. None of these cowboys or sodbusters or women in this story ever were advised by an artist in regard to anything they would wear. They didn't have western costume companies to make them look attractive and conspicuous.

"I make this point strong because it seems everybody's effort is to make them look as much like western movie actors as possible. The most difficult job we have is to imagine the people so they will look like any group of people we would see if we parachuted down into a location like this in the northwest in 1890."

The *Saturday Evening Post* wrote about Stevens, "Convinced he works better under pressure, he creates pressure around him. With this in mind he keeps his staff and crew in a state of tension."

As the summer dragged on, *Shane* went over budget and behind schedule. Worried that they were paying too much money for a standard Ladd movie, studio representatives started poking around, which infuriated Stevens.

During *The Member of the Wedding* Brandon jumped around on a stage for an hour and a half with people he loved then basked in applause. Out here, a typical work day called him out of his hotel room at 8:30 a.m. and often not back to his room until after 7:00 p.m., sometimes not getting to say one line.

But there were compensations.

George Stevens arranged for a saddle horse to be available to Brandon while he was in Wyoming so he could ride whenever he wasn't needed on the set. With the horse came a cowboy hat and western boots, and leather chaps hand-tooled with his name. And on the train ride back home Stevens gave him a toy for every city the train passed through.

And Brandon got to hang out with Peter Pan. During the run of *The Member of the Wedding* Jean Arthur was a few theaters down the street, playing the boy who never grows up. He saw the show on a night off and was captivated. When he went backstage to meet her, Boris Karloff told him she was sick and not receiving visitors, offering the consolation of letting him try on his Captain Hook eye patch.

In Wyoming, the actress told Brandon that she watched *The Member of the Wedding* three times and when Brandon appeared skeptical, she asked, "Do you remember the night you sneezed during the card game?"

Brandon rode horses since the age of five and said in the 1962 book *The Player*, "But now instead of riding on bridle paths I could ride in the wide open spaces. On weekdays when I wasn't working my parents, Jean Arthur, and some wranglers I knew and I went horse-back riding and I used to imagine that we were cowboys in the old west."

Alan Ladd's stepdaughter Carol Lee told a magazine reporter that Brandon "drove all the actors a little crazy because his idea of fun was jumping up and down in the mud and splashing it all over everyone." Sometimes when Brandon was shooting a solemn scene Jean Arthur positioned herself behind Stevens' back and made funny faces. She would also get him to hide when the director needed him. Ben Johnson, who plays a cattle rancher who switches over to the good side, remembered frantic searches for him.

The last scene in *Shane*, between Brandon deWilde and Alan Ladd, is one of the most heartrending ever filmed.

Shane has killed the powerful cattle baron Luke Fletcher as well as Fletcher's gun-for-hire played by Jack Palance, and thanks to Joey's cry of "Shane! Look out!" narrowly escapes death himself by killing a third gunman who emerges from a balcony doorway. The valley is safe again. He wearily mounts his horse.

"Can't I ride home behind you?"

"I'm afraid not Joey"

"Please, why not?"

"I gotta be going on."

"Why, Shane?"

"A man has to be what he is, Joey. He can't break the mold. I tried it; it didn't work for me."

"We want you, Shane."

"Joey, there's no living with a killing. There's no going back from it. Right or wrong, it's a brand, and a brand sticks.... Now you run home to your mother. Tell her everything's all right. Tell her there's no more guns in the valley.

"You go home to your mother and father and grow up to be strong, and straight. And Joey, take care of them. Both of them."

He rides off into the inky-blue night, and Brandon runs a

few steps after him, stops and crows out, "They never would have been able to shoot you if you had seen them!" A few more steps and then another stop. "He never would have cleared the holster, would he, Shane?"

A sprint, then the shouted words as Shane rides further away: "Pa's got things for you to do! And mother wants you. I know she does. Shaaane!" A close-up of Joey's dirt-smudged face registers the confusion and intensity of a child suffering his first heartbreak, and his words echo over Victor Young's majestic score as Shane, stooped because his arm was hit by a bullet, rides out of the valley, shrinking ever smaller in the distance. "Shaaane...come back!"

According to a newspaper report at the time, every time Ladd spoke his lines of farewell Brandon crossed his eyes and stuck out his tongue. Finally, Ladd called to Fritz, "Make that kid stop or I'll beat him over the head with a brick."

Shooting and past-production wrapped up on October 13. Brandon and his mother were two of the three hundred cast, crew, and family members who attended a party thrown by Alan Ladd and Jean Arthur in Hollywood on October 16th, 1951. But Paramount didn't feel festive.

George Stevens Jr. told the author that Paramount Studios tried to sell the film to Howard Hughes [then owner of the RKO studio] for cost. "They knew an Alan Ladd film never made more than $2.6 million and this one cost about three million." And Gene Autry, Roy Rogers, the Lone Ranger, and the Cisco Kid could be watched, free, at home so why would moviegoers pay to watch a western? George Stevens, Jr. said the executives didn't appreciate that his father was "making something distinctive, not like the last western they made."

While the director burrowed into the editing room, his film was written off by the studio and shelved.

5

A class act

At least two individuals in Baldwin were excited about how Brandon spent his summer. "It was a very big deal for me at the time that I should get a gun and holster from Alan Ladd," said Kenneth Schmidt. Greg Murphy remembered Brandon bringing home "arrows with rubber tips, a couple of guns. When we went off to play cowboys and Indians, we went armed."

For a fourth grade class assignment, Richard Burns and Brandon decided to make a space station out of construction paper at Brandon's house. "He told me one of his parents' friends were going to be there," said Burns, now an attorney, "and mentioned that her name was Jean Arthur. I remember telling my mom that, and her saying, 'well you have to get dressed up nicely.' And I remember saying, 'I'm not going for an audition, I'm just going for a science project.'" The actress, Burns recalled, "dressed us up as space cadets and took pictures of us."

Kenneth Schmidt said that Brandon was, "hit and miss in school. He'd be there for six weeks and then he was gone again." So it happened late that fall when he was pulled into rehearsals for *Mrs. McThing*. The play was slated to open at the

Martin Beck Theater on February 20, 1952 for a two-week run as a benefit for a non-profit theater group started by Robert Whitehead. The producer told the author that a main reason he settled on this particular play was that, "there was a very good part for a little boy."

Brandon's character, Howay, is introduced on stage by a life-size oil painting. "This boy has blond hair and mischievous blue eyes," wrote the playwright Mary Chase. "He looks as though he would like to jump out of the painting, and play cops and robbers, run, yell and jump over chairs. But he doesn't. He stands silently and proudly, like a young prince."

A six-foot rabbit starred in Chase's 1946 Pulitzer Prize-winning *Harvey*, and *Mrs. McThing* shared its whimsical vein. Howay turns out to be an irrepressibly naughty boy who is forbidden to play with a witch's daughter. The witch conjures up an insufferably well-behaved version of Howay, and in the end, Howay's snobby mother swears never again to turn her nose up at anyone and, missing her bad but fun son, decides it's best to let boys be boys.

Brandon's mother was played by Helen Hayes, who was considered the first lady of the American theater. Ernest Borgnine had a small part, three years before his career exploded at the age of thirty-eight with the role of a kind-hearted butcher named Marty. Fred Gwynne, later chief Munster on TV, made his theatrical debut. Bobby Mariotti was Brandon's understudy again, and the witch's daughter was played by seven-year-old Lydia Reed, later star of the TV show *The Real McCoys*.

Brandon played both Howays and was on stage for seventy minutes. Genie helped him negotiate his many costume changes from good boy to bad, and she was also his makeup artist. For Fritz, this was the second in a string of some twenty Broadway plays he would go on to manage.

Brandon took the pile of opening-night telegrams in stride this time. The only one that got him excited was from Mary Martin, who was on tour in London with *South Pacific*. Brandon had watched the show a half dozen times on Broadway and spent more than ten weeks worth of allowance on the soundtrack album.

"Broadway's biggest freak success since P.T. Barnum presented Tom Thumb," is how *Mrs. McThing* was proclaimed in a morning newspaper. The closing date was ripped open and so was the date when Brandon would be on a regular public school schedule again.

Brandon's teacher Helene Light said that during the run of *Mrs. McThing*, "I would give him my noon hour and work with him on all his lessons that he would be missing. He knew I had a son who was about the same age. He said, 'Oh, I'd like to meet him.' So I said, 'Someday at noon, instead of working in the classroom, I'll take you home with me.' So I did, and Larry and he had the best time.

"I felt proud. I had my head up. It was something extra for me. I was elated about it because, oh, here's a boy so popular on the stage and everything, and I have a part in educating him."

The March 10, 1952 edition of *LIFE* featured early campaigning in New Hampshire by presidential nominees Eisenhower and Taft, and Jane Russell, Yvonne de Carlo, and Miss Denise Lawson-Johnston "of New York and London Society" in evening gowns and hawking, respectively, Sylvania radio and TV repair, the Ayds reducing plan, and Herbert Tareyton cigarettes.

The cover was given over to ten-year-old Brandon, cockily leaning back on an elbow, his thumb and middle finger forming a circle, wearing a bowler hat and the oversize, pin-striped suit of Howay the Bad.

A theater critic called Brandon "every inch an actor. He has never taken a lesson in elocution or dramatics but has an instinctive genius for feeling the emotions and moods of a scene and for projecting them to an audience." Helen Hayes marveled how "he never forgets a line or misses a cue."

The competition on Broadway that season for a theatergoer's $1.75 included Katharine Hepburn in *The Millionairess*, Bette Davis in a musical revue, Patricia Neal and Kim Hunter in *A Children's Hour*, John Garfield in *Golden Boy*, and Tom Ewell in *The Seven Year Itch*.

Julie Harris was a few stage doors down from Brandon as Sally Bowles in *I Am a Camera*, for which she won her first of a record five Tony Awards (not including a special Tony for Life Achievement in the theater that she and Robert Whitehead won in 2002) and for which Walter Kerr wrote his famous review, "I no Leica."

Also on Broadway, in a hit one-woman show, was the English comedienne Beatrice Lillie. Lillie had visited backstage after seeing *Mrs. McThing*, and she and Brandon exchanged autographed photos plus rode his go-cart together down Westminster Road in Baldwin and a boat through the Tunnel of Love in Palisades Amusement Park. Newspapers quoted Lillie saying she usually hated child actors but "this one I love. He doesn't act. He just walks out on stage and behaves like a boy you wish was yours."

Helen Hayes became close with Brandon's family, putting them up in her Manhattan flat when they were between apartments and having them to dinner at her home in Nyack, New York. While Helen and her husband, James MacArthur, chatted with Fritz and Genie, Brandon and their thirteen-year-old son puffed cigarettes in the basement.

The play was Hayes's biggest Broadway success to date and she played Mrs. Larue for two years, taking the show on the road in January of 1953. Brandon said, "I never got bored while I was doing it, any more than I did while I was in my first play. I'm never bored onstage." But he had to leave the stage for the movies after the play's six-month run on Broadway: Rehearsals began for the movie version of *The Member of the Wedding* on June 9, and shooting two weeks after that.

* * *

In the 1930s and '40s, the American movie was synonymous with Hollywood. But in the 1950s, movies with shoestring budgets and offbeat talents began popping up, treating unique subjects in an honest way. Two movies from 1952 and 1953 personified this trend: *Little Fugitive,* which was shot from the perspective of a little boy who believes that in some playful gunplay he killed someone, and *The Member of the Wedding.*

Fred Zinnemann said that when he fell in love with the play and decided to film it, "one of my ambitions was to retain the extraordinary affection which tied the three principal actors together." Ethel Waters had been nominated (with Ethel Barrymore) for a Best Supporting Actress Academy Award for her role in Elia Kazan's *Pinky* two years earlier. But Julie and Brandon had not yet appeared on movie screens and Zinnemann had to battle with Columbia Pictures to keep them.

The actors who played Frankie's father and Berenice's fiance were back. Jus Addiss was brought in as Ethel Waters's dialogue coach. "Addiss got on well with Ethel," Whitehead wrote to Zinnemann in recommending him for the job, adding, "Although in those early days she was somewhat less formidable."

Zinnemann wrote to Carson McCullers that the scriptwriters, Edna and Edward Anhalt, followed the play "in almost every respect, with the only deviations as are necessary to establish the mood and atmosphere of the world and town outside."

He wrote to Whitehead that the script "is based almost exclusively on the effectiveness of dialogue rather than any imaginative visual treatment which might have derived from the novel. I feel it's the best we can hope for. I'm very grateful we are at least following the spirit of the play instead of tampering with it or inserting extraneous material."

A month before shooting started, he wrote McCullers, "My only regret is that my main ambition will not be realized—to make a motion picture. But the film will come off in similar terms and for the same reasons that the play did. …The fact that a great deal more could have been done is something I must now dismiss from my mind so I can concentrate on doing the best possible job within the limitations."

Brandon and Genie spent the Fourth of July at a pool party at the home of Gary Merrill, an army friend of Fritz's, and Merrill's wife, Bette Davis. The couple was celebrating the wrap of *All About Eve*. Brandon invited Julie Harris. He was dazzled by the fireworks, which were illegal in Baldwin: she, by Bette. "I was so in awe of her," Julie recalled. She also remembered Merrill walking out onto the diving board dressed in his officer's uniform and jumping into the water: "The kids were thrilled that a grown-up would do that."

The five-week location shooting for *The Member of the Wedding* was in Colusa by the Sacramento River in central California, which looked more like the sleepy south of the 1940s than the actual south, which had become heavily industrialized since the war.

Zinnemann tweaked the script to reflect Brandon being two years older than when he played the part on Broadway; for instance, having him smack the doll that Frankie gives him instead of kissing it.

He wanted to alter the ending of the play, where John Henry dies, because he felt the audience would be very attached to Brandon's John Henry and also because in the original theater production some critics had taken exception to the sudden death, considering it "an unfair trick."

But Whitehead argued strongly in a letter to the director for keeping the original ending. "There is a grey lonely feeling of autumn. The start of a new chapter in Frankie's life and the fact that she remembers his death as the week of the fair and her meeting with Mary at the lipstick counter at Woolworth, the beginning of superficiality. It all brings for me a deep human truth, comic yet tragic. I feel I know John Henry must die. Carson's deepest talent is an intuitive ability to recall. John Henry's death is part of a whole truth and as such cannot be any other way."

The movie came out in December 1952. "There is a wide divergence in public and critical acceptance, with reactions divided between people who hate the picture passionately and are almost hysterical in their praise," Zinnemann wrote McCullers in its second week. "The only certain thing seems to be that it will not be a great money maker."

The Member of the Wedding made *TIME*'s list of the ten best movies of 1952 along with *Come Back Little Sheba, Singin' in the Rain,* and *The Quiet Man*. Al Hine of *Holiday Magazine* wrote Zinnemann that he "did what I thought was damn near impossible—made a great movie out of a great play without either slavishly copying or joking it up for the popcorn trade." The writer James Agee told Zinnemann, "I cried gallons and felt no need to be ashamed of one tear."

John Mason Brown, the critic for the *Saturday Review,* wrote it was "in the nature of a public service to have Julie's extraordinary performance preserved on screen. As for Brandon, he continues to show that he is a remarkable boy actor, one quite removed from the usual Hollywood monstrosity who is either sickish sweet or too cute for words."

On the negative side, *Variety* opined, "the art house should find it as rewarding dramatically as the play, but to the regular run of filmgoers it will be an 88-minute conversation piece, more soporific than stimulating." *The New York Times'* Bosley Crowther called Brandon "a little lanky in the legs" for the role.

Robert Whitehead's viewpoint was somewhere in the middle. He thought the movie, while respectful of his play "to the point of being a record for the files," "lacked the spontaneity, breadth, smell and feeling of life" of live theater. But he said when he ran a 16 mm print many years later, "Strangely enough, I quite loved it."

In 1979, Zinnemann wrote a film student that whether the movie should have followed the book or the play "is a moot question. The film is what it is with Carson's wonderful dialogue preserved intact. Whatever regrets I had have long since disappeared." He went on to direct *Oklahoma!* and his *From Here to Eternity* and *High Noon*, which sandwiched *The Member of the Wedding*, won a total of twelve Oscars. He called *The Member of the Wedding* "my biggest flop and my favorite film."

* * *

Brandon was cast in Robert Whitehead's third consecutive Broadway play, prompting a reporter for *The New York Times* to say about the producer that "besides considering Brandon deWilde a capable young actor, there is the chance he regards him as a lucky omen."

Brandon's role in *The Emperor's Clothes* wasn't as colorful as the previous two, according to Whitehead, but "it was a good part and a necessary part." The eleven-year-old, according to the playwright's notes, played "a pale, handsome, lovable child of 13 with eyes so darkly intense they obviously contain a refuge of fantastic dreams." His costars were Maureen Stapleton and Lee J. Cobb, three years after he defined Willie Loman in *Death of a Salesman*.

Harold Clurman and Lester Polakov were on board, as director and lighting and set designer respectively, and John Anderson had a small acting role. Fritz was back, too. The elder deWilde's connection with Whitehead was as fortuitous as the younger one's. "Fritz was one of the best stage managers in New York," Robert Whitehead said some forty years later, "and became so largely through the work he did for me. I got to know him because of Brandon but he was a theater person and I quickly used him because I liked him and because he was intelligent and able.

"Finally he ran the stage management department of my office, which was more active in those days." Original Broadway productions that list Frederic deWilde as stage manager include *Bus Stop*, *A Man for All Seasons* and *Come Blow Your Horn*.

Lyle Bettger, an actor and army buddy of Fritz's, said in a letter to the author, "I always felt Fritz began to believe he was very limited in the things he could play and get jobs for as an actor and finally when the opportunity presented itself he grabbed the chance to go into the management and as a stage manager. When I saw the success he was having, and I was still struggling, I said to my wife, 'I shoulda become a stage manager and not had to hack all this shit that actors do.'"

Emperor's Clothes reflects the Red-baiting hysteria fanned by Senator Eugene McCarthy that by 1953 had cleaved the country for three years. The play is set in Budapest and concerns a teacher, played by Cobb, fired ten years before for taking a dangerous political position and who now wants his job back. Brandon said in *The Player* that "It was the first time that I began to understand what I was doing as an actor."

At the play's Detroit preview the critics predicted that it might be too cerebral to attract a large audience. Two weeks after opening night on Broadway, the Ethel Barrymore Theater that hosted the play was dark.

"Superficial," "glib," and "confused" were some of the adjectives hurled by critics with the *International News Service* referencing James M. Cain's first novel with, "The postman doesn't come twice for Lee J. Cobb after his shining success in *Death of a Salesman*."

The one-dimensionality that would later plague Brandon was foreshadowed by one newspaper critic's barb that, "The youngster regarded by many reviewers as only waiting to grow up a little to be another Edmund Kean [a great English tragic actor of the early 1800s], plays the enthralled devotee of Buffalo Bill, Hoot Gibson and Scarlet Pimpernel as if still playing the prissy sissy in *Mrs. McThing*."

But that was just about the only discouraging word. The critic for the *Detroit News* wrote, "Brandon deWilde is a wonder. He meets any acting need required and is also able to cultivate a repose beyond any child actor I ever saw." His old New York

City admirer Brooks Atkinson said, "unsmiling, innately honest, Brandon is altogether superb. It is easy to believe him because he believes in what he is doing." John Chapman, writing in the *Daily News*, said he "continues to grow as an actor." And the *Journal American*'s John McClain called him "frighteningly adept."

"Within four crowded years," recapped Arthur Gelb in the December 1953 *New York Times*, "this blond-thatched prodigy has grown from 49 to 56 inches, enlarged his bulk from 62 to 81 pounds, increased his weekly salary from $150 to a very respectable four figures and upped his allowance from 50 cents to one dollar a week."

The deWildes' standard response when asked what the future held for their son was that he would quit when he was twelve. "By that time he'll have enough in the bank to see him through prep school, college, and a few years afterwards. Of course it's all exciting for him and he loves the people he meets. But it's too hard on him. He's missed out on a lot of things. He has to be tutored an hour for every half day of school he misses. If he wants to be an actor after he grows up that's up to him. But he's not going to say to us, 'you got me into this.'"

That plan might still have seemed sound in March of 1953, when Brandon was eleven. But not in April when he turned twelve: Paramount was releasing *Shane*.

Photo Gallery
#1

While Brandon was posing for this second grade class picture, a Broadway director was looking for "a boy who will melt your heart." Brandon is in the center of the front row and his friend Richard Burns is at the far right of this row. *Photo courtesy of Richard Burns.*

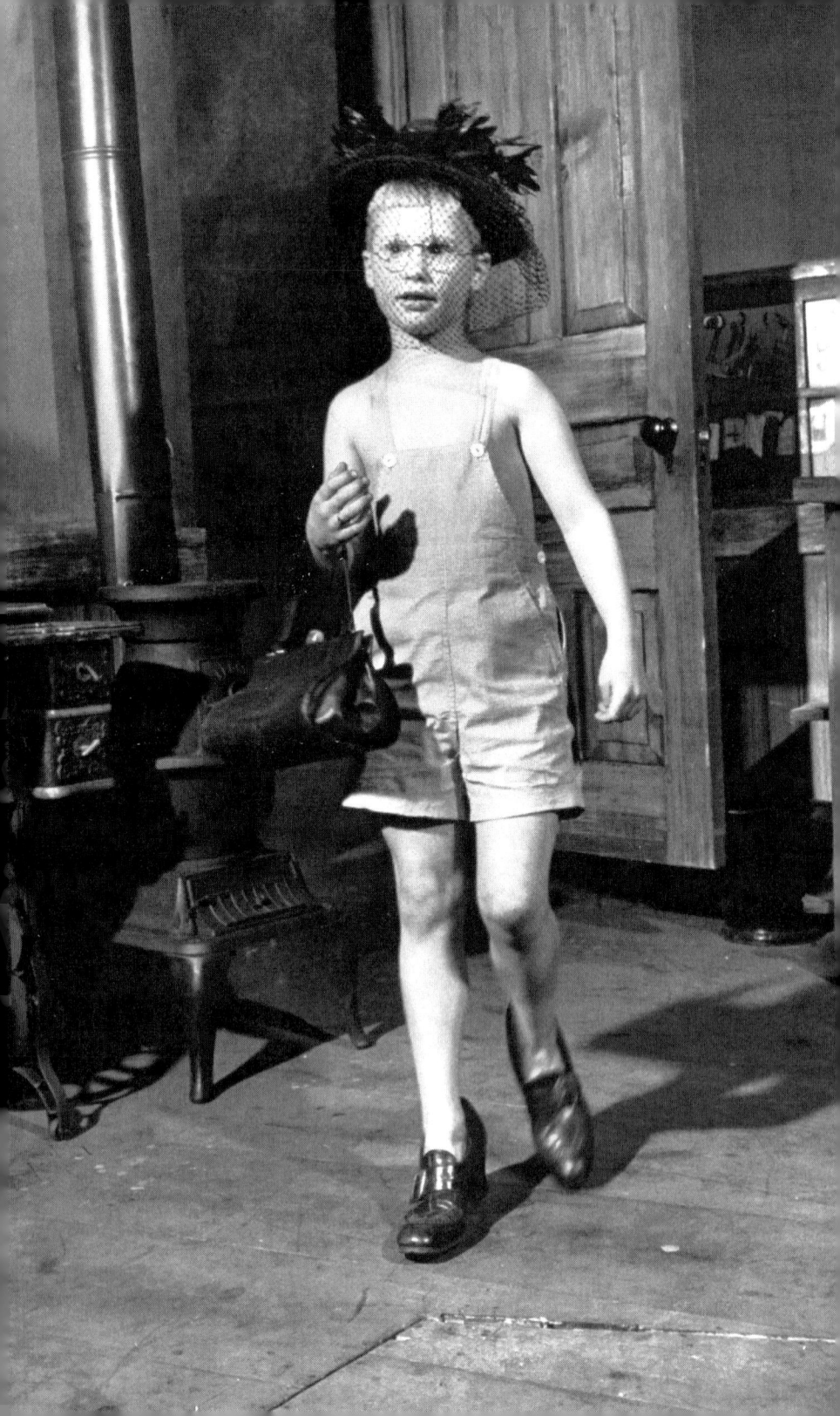

"We just loved each other and took care of each other, and enjoyed being together," Julie Harris said of the three stars of *The Member of the Wedding*.

"It certainly didn't help his standing in the neighborhood," said a friend from Baldwin about this LIFE Magazine photo of Brandon on stage in *The Member of the Wedding*. *Eliot Elisofon/Time&LIFE Pictures/Getty Images*

When Brandon made the cover of LIFE, he was starring with Helen Hayes in his second hit Broadway show. *Shane* was a year from being released. *Nina Leen/ Time&LIFE Pictures/Getty Images*

During third and fourth grade Brandon starred in his second Broadway show, in two movies, and in many television shows. *Photos courtesy of Richard Burns.*

Brandon's father was his acting coach from the very beginning. Here, they study lines together on the movie set of *The Member of the Wedding*.
©1952 Columbia Pictures Corp. Photo by Van Pelt.

The daughter of Gary Merrill (army buddy of Brandon's father and Brandon's future co-star) and Bette Davis, hanging out with Brandon on the movie set of *The Member of the Wedding*.
©1952 Columbia Pictures Corp. Photo by Van Pelt.

Brandon and his father play with the model train set in their basement, "the most magnificent one you've ever seen," according to a family friend. *Collection of Tony Reznak, Jr.*

The portrait of Brandon was by the set designer of the Broadway show that made Brandon a star. Brandon's mother, Genie, said the dreamy quality "reflected the deWilde state of mind at the time." *Collection of Tony Reznak, Jr..*

C2034

CATTLE RANCH IN TETON VALLEY, WYOMING

Here in the unsurpassed natural beauty of "The last of the old West" hospitable guest ranches play host each summer to vacationers from all parts of the country.

Dear Greg,
this is where I a[m] making the pictu[re]. Everyplace we go the[re] are horses and cowbo[ys]. See you soon.
Love,
Brando[n]

Mike Roberts for
., Salt Lake City 1, Utah

Master Gregory Murphy
2 Stratford Road
Baldwin, L. I.
New York

Collection of Gregory Murphy.

The New York Times looked past Alan Ladd, Van Heflin, and Jean Arthur to credit 11-year-old Brandon for "stealing the affection of the audience" and clinching *Shane* as "a most unusual film."

© 1953 *Paramount Pictures Corporation.*

© 1953 Paramount Pictures Corporation.

Brandon helps his stand-in Binnie Graefe, a local Wyoming boy, celebrate his birthday on the movie set. *Photo courtesy of Walt Farmer.*

"He's an actor through and through," said Ernest Truex—who had co-starred with Mary Pickford in the 1920s. Brandon was one of the first actors to have his own TV show and Truex played his grandfather.

By the time the 1955 Lenox School yearbook came out, with Brandon's seventh grade photo, he had already transferred to the Professional Children's School in New York City. *Photo courtesy of Richard Burns.*

By 1953, in an era when most American adults had never flown in an airplane, Brandon had taken twenty-three flights. Maarten Heybroek, who visited family in Europe frequently, said, "I flew the Constellation and Strata Cruiser to Holland and he flew the DC 6 to California."

In 1956, Brandon spent two weeks at summer camp in Maine. His best friend Maarten Heybroek is the fifth boy from Brandon in the same row and toward the center. This same year Brandon co-starred with Walter Brennan in the movie *Goodbye My Lady* and with *The Bad Seed*'s Patty McCormack on TV. *Photo courtesy of Maarten Heybroek.*

On a break from filming *Goodbye My Lady*.

Night Passage with James Stewart.

Wed. 18, 1950

The Grand Imperial Hotel
OWNED AND OPERATED BY THE TEXAS HOUSING COMPANY
Silverton, Colorado

Dear Greg,

(ROTH) How are you? Boy, am I having fun up here. We have been working on the picture about a week now. I have been pretty busy (not busy enough to keep from writing to Linda twice) (she wrote me to) The picture is coming along pretty well. I am a real cowboy — Boots, Jeans, wide belt, plaid shirt, neckerchief and hat. I ride a horse, get shot, and live with the bad men (Audie Murphy and his gang) Jimmy Stewart and Audie Murphy are real good guys. I have a 45 and holster between scenes and I am pretty fast on the draw.   over —

I can ride my horse any time I want.
The picture is being made with every thing — steriophony sound fishyvision, and tickle color. No, its really made with everything though. Every thing you can dream of. (hork)
My hair is pretty long.
We use a real narrow gauge train in the picture that is the last in the good old U.S.
I saw "The Last Wagon" with Richard Widmark. Its real neat, you have too see it.
If the ink seems different its because its the next day now and I have to go to work. (ZORCH)
I'll see you when I get back, and write to me to the address on the back of the envelope, see you

Brandon

A letter to Greg Murphy from the set of *Night Passage*. Murphy said the year at the top of the letter is a mistake and that Brandon's asides in parentheses are references to the *Steve Allen Show* and *Mad Magazine*. Collection of Gregory Murphy.

Brandon appeared in a sketch with *Wizard of Oz*'s Bert Lahr and character actor Eddie Mayehoff in 1957 in a 90-minute special on NBC called the Standard Oil Anniversary Show. The host was Tyrone Power, guests included Jimmy Durante, Jane Powell, Donald O'Conner and Duke Ellington, and Brandon's name was first on the publicity program.

6

King of the child stars

The most famous child actor of the 1980s looked a lot like the Brandon of three decades earlier. The writer-director John Hughes told the *New York Times* that at test screenings for *Uncle Buck*, the nine-year-old making his movie debut "had an extraordinary effect on people. Every card came back, 'Favorite thing in the movie—the little boy.' I knew I'd stumbled onto something." And then came the highest-grossing comedy in movie history, and Macaulay Culkin's follow-up, *Home Alone*.

Star quality was as evident for Brandon in the test screening of *Shane*. In a dozen dense pages of comments from audience members, there was nitpicking about Alan Ladd, the genre, and the booming soundtrack, but Brandon's name burns like Sirius in a night sky. "Who is the little boy? He was outstanding." "I think he is going places." "He stole the show." "Boy excellent." "Expressive eyes." "Little Joey a natural actor." "Kid is wonderful." "Little boy the most interesting part of the picture." "Liked the little boy." "Hope we see more of him." "The only one who was good was the cross-eyed kid and the dog."

Greg Murphy was the lucky friend invited to join Brandon at the world premiere of *Shane* on April 23, 1953, at Radio

City Music Hall in New York City. The two fourth graders also stopped by the celebrity hang out Toots Shor for a children's party in Brandon's honor. A month later, Brandon boarded his twenty-sixth airplane with his parents for the west coast premiere of *Shane* at Grauman's Chinese Theater, where guests included Cary Grant, Joan Fontaine, and Irene Dunne.

On May 26, there was another preview at the Riverview Theater in Norfolk, hometown of the book's author. It was Genie's hometown, too, and her parents and sister still lived there. Genie's family, the Wilsons, sat with the Riverview Theater manager and a reporter named Warner Twyford from the *Norfolk Virginian-Pilot*. "With Brandon's forlorn, wistful farewell echoing in our ears, we gathered in the lobby," wrote Twyford. "His aunt thought it was wonderful, so did her youngsters. His grandmother was weeping, 'The picture was so sad,' but she soon got over it and beamed with happiness at Brandon's success. But she insisted that she was happy because Brandon is such a normal, unspoiled little boy. 'His parents never were ambitious for him to be an actor, and we really don't care about an acting career for him. It's fine that he can do so well, and that he likes it, but we'd be just as proud of him anyway.'"

Variety lifted the curtain on *Shane* by writing, "Socko drama with both class and mass appeal. Strong box office possibilities." And this line, from a three-page spread on the movie a few years later in *LOOK*, reflected the general tone at the time of the film's release: "*Shane* will take its place in motion picture history as one of the greatest westerns of them all, side by side with *Stagecoach*, *The Searchers* and *High Noon*."

Alan Ladd got the best reviews of a seventy-movie career, with one critic saying he gave the best performance ever of a western hero. "He repeats his standard characterization," said another. "But his good bad man is credible, as if the character Ladd has created so often on the screen has at last been traced to its authentic origins."

The *New York Times* critic looked past Ladd, Van Heflin, and

Jean Arthur, and the character actors Jack Palance, Ben Johnson, and Elisha Cook, and laid the movie's success at the feet of a twelve-year-old. "It is Master deWilde," Bosley Crowther wrote, "with his bright face, clear voice, and resolute boyish ways who steals the affection of the audience and clinches *Shane* as a most unusual film."

Three days after the New York City movie premiere, the spotlight was again on Brandon in a highly acclaimed ABC *Plymouth Playhouse* episode called "Jamie" where he played a seven-year-old orphan taken in by his lovable grandfather.

Fritz deWilde joined forces with two of Hollywood's most esteemed television producers to find a worthy television series for his son. Julian Claman was behind *Have Gun Will Travel*, and David Susskind was the Robert Whitehead of TV, with his reputation for mounting productions that were as artistic as they were successful.

The trio pitched a show based on *Jamie* to ABC, and the studio signed Brandon to a contract for a comedy series at eighteen hundred dollars a week.

Ernest Truex was brought back as the grandfather. The veteran character actor with twinkly eyes had teamed up with Mary Pickford in 1914 and would appear in two classic episodes of Rod Serling's *Twilight Zone*, "Kick the Can" and "What You Need." He told the *Saturday Evening Post* for the feature article about Brandon, "The Star Who'd Rather Play Marbles," in May 1954, "You ask him to do anything—joy, disappointment, frustration, misery, loneliness, any damn thing—and this kid can get it across. And he doesn't depend on cuteness for his effects. He knows exactly what he's doing. He's a thinking actor. Once he's fixed on a reading of a line or a bit of business during rehearsals he's sure to come through perfectly on the actual performance. Usually with kid actors you're nervous and jumpy, figuring you have to cover up for them in case they start flubbing, but with this kid you always feel secure. He's just a natural, just born that way—an actor through and through."

Brandon garnered a lot of adulatory press coverage for having a TV show written for him, the fourth person so honored after Ray Bolger, Ezio Pinza, and Danny Thomas. But because Brandon was the youngest person to hold this honor, a flurry of editorials questioned whether a child, no matter how well-adjusted, could handle the pressure and workload. Brandon skipped about half the rehearsals so that he could stay in public school, and a clause was written into his contract letting him leave the show at any time if he or his parents thought the pressure too much.

"Based on the daily events in the life of an 11-year-old," wrote Arthur Gelb in the December 27, 1953, *New York Times*, "the comedy borrows liberally from the young actor's own offstage activities. And since it hopes to continue on the airwaves indefinitely it plans to have Jamie MacHummer's chronological age keep pace with Brandon's own." Brandon helped draw this parallel by arranging for his friend Greg Murphy to be cast in a couple of episodes.

While the writers hammered out scripts for *Jamie*, Brandon was sent out to publicize both the TV series and *Shane*.

In Washington, DC, he was photographed shaking hands with J. Edgar Hoover. According to the *Chicago Tribune Magazine*, Brandon told the FBI director that he wanted to be a G-Man, and Hoover let him shoot a machine gun.

Back home in Baldwin, Ed Murrow came calling with his fifteen-person crew for the TV show *Person to Person*. Brandon was also the mystery guest on the January 10, 1954, edition of *What's My Line?* Here, a panel of sophisticated New York media stars in tuxedos, evening gowns, and black eye masks try to guess the identity of a celebrity disguising his or her voice. Brandon spoke in a throaty drawl, and Bennett Cerf asked, "You are human, of course?" after Arlene Francis finally established that the guest was a star of theater and movies and "even younger than eighteen." The host, John Daly, stepped in for a demurring Brandon to answer in the affirmative the final question, "Might you be considered one of the boy wonders of the American stage today?" In March, Brandon and Audrey Hepburn posed with their respective LOOK Magazine statuettes (his was for *Shane*, hers for *Roman Holiday*) at the thirteenth annual film achievement award ceremony in Hollywood hosted by Eddie Cantor.

That particular summer, Brandon could only get away to Camp Mitigwa in Rangeley, Maine, for two weeks. He and Maarten Heybroek had previously spent whole summers there, in a tradition that Heybroek said started with their parents' fear of the polio epidemic and its easier communicability in the New York summer heat.

The live telecast of *Jamie* debuted on September 28 and did well in its Monday 7:30 p.m. slot between Walter Winchell and *Sky King* and opposite Perry Como's variety show and *Arthur Murray's Dance Party*, the precursor to Dick Clark's *American Bandstand*.

Bruce Laffey said that with *Jamie*, Brandon started encountering autograph seekers when he left Baldwin. "He would get so embarrassed. He was always very nice to them, but it was, like, 'What's that all about?'"

Julian Claman, producer of *Jamie* as well as *Have Gun Will Travel*, told a reporter, "Most kid actors get by because they're cute. Well, there's no phony cuteness about Brandon. He hasn't been sugarcoated to make him salable. He's so natural he could be anybody's kid down the block. And to be natural on the stage or in front of a camera may look easy, but it takes the greatest acting skill."

Brandon got his usual truckload of respect from the critics. Harriet Van Horne of the *New York World-Telegram* was ambivalent about the first episode but not about Brandon. "He's far too professional to have any of those hideous child-actor mannerisms, the brattish traits that always register twice life-size on TV. He is quiet, quick, and full of purpose, like a well-brought-up little cat. He doesn't pout or posture. And when he grins, his solemn, intelligent face takes on a kind of grubby ecstasy. There were many touching moments in this slow, but an over-plotted story. There was an air of nice, homely goodness too. But the genuineness of young deWilde showed up every false turn of the story, every mawkish line. It also put to shame some overacting by the rest of the cast."

Truex and co-star Polly Rowles, she wrote, while first-rate, "should count themselves lucky to be working with so distinguished an actor as Master deWilde."

One of the afternoons when he was in school, a photographer for the magazine *The American* showed up. Helene Light said, "He took pictures of him as a normal boy coming into school like all other children. They had to put on their coats and pretend they were going home, and he was to be with them when he walked out. Of course, then they had to come in and take their coats off, and they all said 'oh! Why can't we go home?'"

To make up for lost school time, Brandon spent four hours a week with a state-authorized tutor. He seemed to prove the doubters wrong as he ably juggled the show and schoolwork.

The year the theme song for a show about a coonskin-capped frontiersman named Davy Crockett sold four million records, Brandon rode in the Macy's Day Thanksgiving parade. He waved to hundreds of thousands of people lining Fifth Avenue, along with William Boyd and his sidekick Gabby Hayes, Buffalo Bob Smith, Imogene Coca and Sid Caesar, Wally Cox, Celeste Holm, Martha Raye, Steve Allen, Faye Emerson, and Eddie Fisher.

On February 26, 1953, at the Golden Globes Awards ceremony at the Ambassador Hotel in Los Angeles, special awards were given to John Wayne and Walt Disney, and to Brandon for his role in the movie version of *The Member of the Wedding*.

Also that year, he was nominated for an Oscar in the Best Supporting Actor category for *Shane*—the youngest person ever to be so nominated. He and Jack Palance were nominated in the same category, and concerns that they would cancel each other out proved true as Frank Sinatra, galloping down the comeback trail in *From Here to Eternity*, captured the statuette.

(A later friend, Michael Muentz, said that Brandon, "was really teed off because he believed that Frank Sinatra had switched his category from Best Actor to Best Supporting Actor so he would have a better chance of winning an award.")

Brandon had conquered the theater, movies, and television. In December, columnist Hedda Hopper wrote, "Never in the entire history of movies has there been such remarkable juvenile talent." She cited Tommy Rettig, Patty McCormack, Billy Chapin (who made his film debut in a Gary Cooper movie when he was a few weeks old and eight years later won the 1951 N.Y. Drama Critics Award for most promising young actor of the year), and Sally Jane Bruce (who peaked as an actress that year at the age of five, playing opposite Charles Laughton in the 1955 film noir *Night of the Hunter*). And then she announced: "The king of them all is Brandon deWilde."

* * *

Jamie ended abruptly on October 4, 1954, two weeks into its successful second season, because of disagreements between the network and a sponsor, at a time when companies owned the network time slots during which their shows aired.

Despite the publicity proclaiming that Brandon was handling the pressures of having his own TV series just fine, he later said in *The Player* that it was "too hard. I had to go to school and learn things like geography and arithmetic and learning lines for a new show every week was just too much."

Just as most people describing Brandon's parents mention that they were well-dressed, Brandon's school friends invariably describe him as exuberant. "He was a very outgoing person," said Rick Williams. "There was nothing shy or reticent about him. Loud, arrogant, but a lot of fun."

Around the time of *Jamie*, his mother told a magazine

reporter that Brandon, "seems to make friends with an unusual assortment of grown-ups," citing Boris Karloff, Mary Martin, Tallulah Bankhead, Beatrice Lillie, and Helen Hayes.

"The Double Life of Brandon De Wilde," was the headline of the lead feature story of the May 24, 1953 *New York Times* Sunday magazine, with the subhead, "This child actor is as formidable as any adult onstage; beneath the greasepaint, however, he is all boy." Meyer Berger had interviewed the fifth-grader—who was accompanied by his mother and a Paramount publicist—at Sardi's. The main photo of the feature shows Brandon wrestling with a peer, and he was quoted as saying, "Whenever anybody is mad at me in school it's always, 'Look at the big movie star getting beat up.' There's a kid, Richard Burns. Of course he can't beat me up. He can't beat a thing up. He's smaller than I am, but he says, 'Look at the big shot.'"

Next Sunday's magazine included this letter to the editor: "I am Richard Burns. You put my name in your paper which I did not mind. But I wish you would correct that I could not beat up Master de Wilde. All my friends are making fun of me… these Whittness [sp] are people who saw me win Master de Wilde: Maureen Dee Maisel, James Deutsch, Ronald Deutsch, Carol Curry, Linda Thomson, Douglas Burns, Mike Wolf, John Albin, Gerald Appell, Bette Arelt, Kerry Rutherford, Carole Beckmann, Faith Emmerich, Dianne Blagburn, Dick Perry, Elaine Sulor."

More than a half a century later, Richard Burns characterized the teasing that Brandon got as standard elementary school treatment, adding that he himself was picked on because he was short, and because his mother made him wear a hat to school. But Brandon's fourth grade grade teacher Helene Light said about Brandon, "He was very disliked. He wasn't popular. I remember children criticizing him, and I would say, 'Now wait a moment. Do you remember Elaine?' She was a violinist and was in all our concerts. I would say, 'She has that talent. She has to practice and appear before the public. Brandon has a different art. He wants to be on the stage. Maybe you're a football player.

So everyone has their own likes and you have to like these people for what they're doing.' But then recess would come, and I would look out the window and they would be running after him and pulling his hair."

Florence Reis said, "He talked very well so that made him different. In *Jamie*, when he left in the afternoon some of the kids resented that. They would say, "Well, he can leave now and I can't!" Even mothers resented his fame. I remember one of them saying to me, "Oh, that *Shane* drives me crazy. If I hear *Shane* one more time I'm going to scream."

Kenneth Schmidt, a star athlete on campus, said that Brandon "wasn't a helluva good football, basketball or baseball player. The key to popularity in the '50s was athletics. Kids that couldn't handle that were losers."

Greg Murphy said, "Coming home there would always be group of guys we would have to push our way through. They called him sissy. Then when *Shane* came out they would run after him and call out, 'Come back, Shane!' Every once in a while I'll run into people who claim to have been his friend. I'll think, 'Boy, I never saw you around.'"

According to Maarten Heybroek, "We were playing basketball once and a couple of hoodlums came and put switch blades to our backs. They recognized him and made him say, 'Come back Shane!' then let us go."

Brandon, 1965: *There are bullies in every school. Lots of the kids were my friends, and still are. But I hated a lot of what went on. I got beat up a lot. There was a big football field next to the school, and sometimes while I was walking across it a bunch of kids would come along and say, 'Let's get that actor.' One time in fourth grade, I brought a pocket knife to school. The teacher asked if someone would go to the office to tell the principal, and everyone raised their hand.*

7

Growing up

From 1954 to 1958, Brandon starred in a movie a year. He also starred in a dozen TV dramas and won *TV Guide's* annual Milky Award for best young performer four consecutive times. Brandon's heyday on the small screen spanned the period from the rise of quiz shows to the stampede of the adult Western. In 1955, the number one show was *The $64,000 Question*; in 1958 it was *Gunsmoke*.

It was also the Golden Age of Television, and all of Brandon's early work in this genre was in the shows that earned this phrase: original, hour-long dramas by playwrights like Paddy Chayefsky, and studded with actors like Rod Steiger, Laurence Harvey, Joanne Woodward, and Basil Rathbone. Videotape was not even invented until 1957, so Brandon's best TV work was filmed live.

In December of 1955, Bill Lundigan presented Brandon in *The Day They Gave Babies Away*, a show for CBS's *Climax Theater* that *TV Guide* billed as "a heart-warming story in the true Christmas spirit. Live from Hollywood in color and black and white." In a 1957 Theater Guild presentation of *The Locked Door* he played the son of June Lockhart who resented his new stepfather, Ralph Bellamy. And in March, 1959, for *Alcoa Theater*, he played a teenager running the family cattle ranch who, as the new man of the house, stands up to the Thursday night whippings of his widowed mother, played by Agnes Moorehead. This NBC series was filmed from New York City on Sundays at 9:00 p.m.

Patty McCormack starred with Brandon in another *Climax Theater* show called *An Episode of Sparrows*. When Brandon was thrilling audiences in *Shane*, the three-years-younger McCormack was chilling them, first on Broadway and then in movie theaters, as a bangs-and-braids killer in *The Bad Seed*. Brandon and Patty, both with trademark platinum-blond hair, symbolized the innocence and hope (the Ike years and post-war peace and prosperity) and the dark terror (McCarthy and the atom bomb) of the 1950s.

His first movie after *Shane* was *Goodbye, My Lady*. As in *Jamie*, he was an orphan with a kindly relative, an uncle this time, played by Walter Brennan. Brandon and Brennan also around this time both read selections from Mark Twain for a 1956 LP, with Brandon voicing Huckleberry Finn.

The Lady in the movie title is a rare Basenji breed of dog. The movie, filmed in rural Georgia during Brandon's thirteenth summer, has the child-finds-pet, child-loves-pet, child-loses-pet theme that was a ritual for the children of Hollywood in the 1940s and '50s, from Liz Taylor in *Lassie Come Home* and *National Velvet* to Claude Jarman Jr. in *The Yearling*. A letter from Brandon to the dog's breeder dated August, 1955, reads, "Dear Miss Tudor-Williams, I am so very sorry not to have written before but I was just too busy...I love Lady very much and can't wait until the film is finished so I can take her home."

The *New York Times* wrote that "the acting, director, and screenplay avoid the mawkishness which the subject so readily suggests and turns an incident from the life of a boy into a folk tale of heroic proportions. Brandon brings the youthful artlessness to the character Skeeter which brought him attention in *Shane*."

Director William Wellman further drove up Brandon's stock when he told Hedda Hopper, "I've made eighty-eight pictures, directed some of the greatest— Jimmy Cagney, Gary Cooper, John Wayne, Freddie March among others. But the best actor of them all is Brandon deWilde. He's not good— he's great!"

* * *

When *Jamie* folded, Genie did too in regard to her Twister-like (board game motto—"It ties you up in knots!") efforts to keep Brandon in public school, and at least one aspect of his life normal.

During seventh grade, in February of 1955, Brandon transferred to a progressive, private school called New Lincoln on the Upper West Side of Manhattan. The family relocated to an apartment at 25 East End Avenue, near East Eightieth Street.

But this school still wasn't flexible enough for Brandon, so in the fall of 1956, his parents succumbed to what they had tried so hard and for so long to avoid. At the Professional Children's School, his classmates included Christopher Walken, a 1950s child television actor; Marvin Hamlisch, who had studied music at Julliard from the age of six; and Tuesday Weld, who in four years would be more famous than any of them as the fantasy girl in *The Many Loves of Dobie Gillis*. Brandon lasted until halfway through the ninth grade, getting enough credits to graduate high school through Searing Tutors.

Genie accompanied Brandon on location to the six movies he made before he was eighteen and on their frequent trips to Hollywood for TV shows, booking a suite with kitchenette in the Montecito Hotel, a popular spot for the New York theater crowd. She sifted through the boxes of fan mail that came in every month, reading some of the letters to her friends and answering them all with a signed 8 x 10-inch glossy of Brandon or a personal note.

Fritz was busy running the stage operations for Robert Whitehead's production company, but he continued to moonlight as his son's acting coach. He rehearsed with him in the theater or studio during the day and again at home in the evening.

"Fritz was the reason Brandon acted so well," said Fritz's friend and colleague John Anderson. He said Fritz was the perfect acting coach because he "didn't have any theories to promote" and he was a "very honest and straightforward" actor.

Anderson said the best thing Fritz might have done for Brandon in this capacity was something he didn't do — enroll him in acting lessons. "He knew that most acting teachers are phony-baloney." This sentiment was echoed by Carol Lynley, who at seventeen had made that many TV show appearances. "The good acting schools don't take children under eighteen," she said. "They think that children don't need to learn to act, and they're right. Children act all the time. They take the most outrageous liberties with the truth and believe in what they say and do. All that children can learn about acting is voice projection and how to take direction."

Brandon said in *The Player*: "Everything I've ever done with my father's guidance has turned out to be good. He can explain meanings in a character that are deeper than I'm capable of finding or understanding by myself. I've learned almost everything I know from my father, and when I understand as much about acting as he does, it will be all I need to know.

"From the beginning my father taught me that I had to believe in a character in order to have the audience believe in it. He showed me how I had to feel that I *was* the character. And he told me I must never try to imitate anyone else, even him. I got the idea, in my own way, from the start. I just always knew I was someone else on stage."

In addition to coaching Brandon in acting, Fritz, along with Genie, was his agent. "We are free-lance and independent," Brandon said in *The Player*. "We say no as often as we say yes to movies that come our way. We've turned down at least 150 movies since I started working. All three of us discuss every script that's sent to us. We each read it separately, then we talk about it—usually at dinner. We tear it apart and each of us gives his opinion. We turn down a script if it sounds too Hollywoody— a shallow, ha-ha, yippee thing."

Night Passage was Brandon's next movie after *Goodbye My Lady*. The Western must have looked good on paper, with James Stewart starring and Brandon's character torn between a good brother and a bad one, but in *The Player*, Brandon called it "a mess" and "the biggest cliché picture ever made."

Stewart appeared after *Night Passage* in *Vertigo*, which received mixed notices on its release but by 2012 was named in one critic's poll as the best film of all time. Brandon followed up *Night Passage* with *The Missouri Traveler*. "It was a bag of shit," his costar Gary Merrill told me in the Cape Elizabeth, Maine, home that he once shared with Bette Davis. Brandon played the title character, receiving top billing with Lee Marvin. The producer was millionaire industrialist Cornelius Vanderbilt Whitney, whose previous film was *The Searchers*, the John Wayne—John Ford epic that battles *Shane* for the title of greatest Western ever made.

In the movie, Brandon played an orphan (again!) in the year 1915 who runs away from an orphanage and settles in a small Midwestern town. The community adopts him as he tries to make it as a farmer. Helping and hindering him are a newspaper editor; rich, ornery farmer; and gregarious saloonkeeper. Whitney let Brandon drive his Lincoln Continental around the Hollywood set and ride his Thoroughbred horses in the ring at his Long Island estate.

"C.V. Whitney didn't know his ass from third base," Merrill said. "And then he puts his wife into it and she can't act," he added, about the thirty-one-year-old Phoenix socialite with four children and no acting experience that Whitney cast in a lead part.

Newsweek agreed with Merrill's assessment: "The trouble

with filming a landscape of a sleepy village and a group portrait of its sleepy citizens is that it's apt to turn into a sleepy movie."

In 1958, Brandon returned to Broadway after a five-year hiatus to star in *Comes a Day*. This was his first play that didn't involve Robert Whitehead. Cheryl Crawford and Alan Pakula produced and Brandon's costars included the formidable Judith Anderson; Michael J. Pollard, nine years before *Bonnie and Clyde;* and the future star of *Patton*, George C. Scott.

Brandon played C.D. Lawton, the fifteen-year-old son in a troubled small-town family. The mother tries to regain the family fortune by marrying off her daughter to a rich man, who seems like the perfect prospect until the family discovers, just in time, that he is a deranged killer.

As Brandon had been noticed as a seven-year-old in his first play, so George C. Scott was noticed at thirty-one in this one, with columnist Walter Kerr calling his portrayal of a psychopath "fascinating." Brooks Atkinson wrote about Brandon, "Once the adorable boy in *Member of the Wedding*, he gives a bright, manly performance that is thoroughly enjoyable." But Atkinson reflected the critical consensus of the play itself with the verdict, "Except for the acting there is little that is genuine in this uneven, baffling drama," and the play, which opened in the beginning of November 1958, was closed by Christmas.

Brandon's first onscreen and offscreen romance was with Carol Lynley when they starred in *Blue Denim*, the 1959 Twentieth Century Fox picture about a young couple, a pregnancy, and a contemplated abortion. Their blond, earnest characters as depictions of teenagers in popular culture fell between that year's *Gidget* and *Rebel Without a Cause* of a few years before.

Because of Brandon's work commitments, he had no time to get his driver's license. So, on weekends, Baldwin friend Kenneth Schmidt and his date would pick up Brandon and Carol in the deWildes' snazzy yellow 1958 Oldsmobile 88 convertible that Fritz kept garaged in Baldwin. Maarten Heybroek said this car, a gift to the family from the car company for Brandon's appearance in an advertisement, was the only outward sign of Brandon's elevated financial status he ever saw. According to Greg Murphy, in the boys' middle class Baldwin neighborhood the Oldsmobile "was like having a Rolls Royce."

Brandon bought his own car within the year, a sporty, two-seat black Sunbeam Alpine, and spent an extra three hundred dollars to soup it up. Rick Williams said Brandon was "always drumming his fingers on the table and moving at 180 miles an hour. He was always looking for a good time." He was "an aggressive, fast-moving person" whose driving matched his personality.

Brandon told a reporter for *Seventeen* in May 1962 that when he wanted to take his car up to its top speed he would seek out a policeman and have him supervise him on a drag strip. Not so, according to Williams. "He would drive everywhere but the road. He was a worse driver than I was. Very abusive. Top always down, yelling and screaming. There would be classic *French Connection* chase scenes. When you're seventeen it's just great. I couldn't get enough of it."

In the August 24, 1959, edition of *LIFE* magazine with Jackie Kennedy on the cover and the caption, "A front runner's appealing wife," is a two-page feature on Brandon. The studio still of him from *The Member of the Wedding* wearing Berenice's purse and hat is juxtaposed with a still from *Blue Denim* of him lying down with Carol. Brandon turned seventeen during the filming, and according to *Screen Stories*, Carol surprised him on the set with a birthday cake decorated with "Happy Birthday Marlon Brandon" reflecting her nickname for him. The article explained that Marlon was Brandon's favorite actor.

The play *Blue Denim* broke two rules in Hollywood's Hayes Production Code: an abortion is performed and the topic is discussed at great length. The screenwriter assured reporters he wouldn't succumb to protests by Roman Catholics but the new ending has a now-mature Arthur Bartley intercepting his girlfriend before she reaches the back-alley abortionist and announcing that he'll marry her.

Two years earlier, *Peyton Place* ripped open the curtain of gentility in small-town America to reveal incest, among other taboos, and a year before, posters for *Baby Doll* showed Caroll Baker sultrily sucking her thumb. But abortion was a novel enough subject in mass culture for Twentieth Century Fox to launch what one publicist called "one of the finest and most provocative advertising, publicity, and exploitation campaigns ever, including a free Carol Lynley star-building trailer," which was narrated, incidentally, by Joan Crawford.

The movie poster shows Carol and Brandon looking solemnly at each other above this type: "Ask yourself...how could it happen to Janet...so shy, so young, so very much like yourself! Where did she go wrong...and why...WHY...WHY? And what about the boy...he was really a decent kid...ask his mother, his father, his friends!"

Bosley Crowther wrote that the abortion theme was "exploited in a shamefully clumsy and artificial way. *Blue Denim* demonstrates Hollywood's great difficulty in coping with adult themes while appealing quite consciously to an audience which to a very large extent does not consist of adults. It also reflects an almost subconscious reflex or desire to placate gripes before they even start pressuring."

Brandon described in *The Player* how he prepared for the role. "I study the script for three to four hours a night, alone, in bed. Along with memorizing my lines, I like to make a lot of notes about how I should move or look." His critique of his performance was "good but not good enough. I didn't make a good enough transition from being a boy to the realization that I was going to be a father."

The professional critics were more generous. *Variety* said he "successfully bridges the gap between moppet roles in *Member* and *Shane*. He has grown up with this role, displaying a remarkably engaging personality and intriguing sympathetic earnestness."

Box Office Magazine wrote that the two young stars "have

great futures on the screen." Offscreen, it ended in a year. Greg Murphy recalled Brandon going on to date model and actress Brooke Bundy, "one of those seventeen-year-olds with a twenty-five-year old face and body."

Brandon said about going steady: "It's awful. The girl's always saying 'Why did you look at another girl?' And you're always saying 'Why do you talk to other fellows?' Now I meet a girl and I say, 'We'll date but we'll go out with others. Anything else is impossible.'"

In December 1959, teenagers lapped up *Modern Screen*'s scoops about Fabian's secret girlfriend, Ricky Nelson's "terrible urge" to ride in demolition derbies (which "had Hollywood biting its nails") and the "agony of parting" for G. I. Elvis Presley and his German sweetheart, Vera Tschechowa. Brandon was quoted in that magazine about his type of girl: "One who doesn't wear rouge or too much lipstick or slacks. I like a girl to wear shorts or feminine dresses. I like one who doesn't drink or use bad language (a hell or a dammit isn't too bad). I like one I can sit down with and talk to for hours."

Brandon traded in the glasses he had worn since age nine for contact lenses. Bruce Laffey remembered that while he had teased him in the past about his pudginess by saying, "Brandon, you're getting a little behind in your work," he had thinned out. "He'd come in here and surprise us," Whitehead said in his elegant offices on Fifty-Fifth Street and Broadway. "The years go by quickly as you well know. I would look at him and say, 'God Almighty, I can't believe it.' You try to avoid saying some old cliché about growing up."

The times had changed, too. When Brandon was in Wyoming filming *Shane*, the male singers at the top of the charts were Eddie Fisher, Perry Como, and Tony Bennett. Then came Elvis. In 1956, four of the top ten songs were his, topped by "Hound Dog" and "Don't Be Cruel."

By 1959, Elvis was in the army and the fever of rock was cooled by a phalanx of generic heartthrobs like Fabian and Pat

Boone. Woody Guthrie and The Weavers had created the first folk wave in the early 1950s and the genre was reintroduced in the early 60s by the more camera-friendly Kingston Trio, all in candy-striped shirts, and Peter, Paul and Mary, with the lead singer swinging her long, straight blond hair.

Brandon had fooled around with his father's guitar since the *Jamie* days. The family was now living in the imposing Belnord apartment building at 225 west 86th Street where a teenager lived downstairs who was steeped in the Greenwich Village folk scene.

8

Music Man

"My fault," Michael Muentz said, laughing, about the second defining shift in Brandon's life.

Muentz, two years younger than Brandon, grew up in the Belnord building. When he first saw Brandon in person, Muentz was an 11th grader at the Professional Children's School, which Brandon had earlier "left, been kicked out of, whatever. Brandon, was walking his dog, the Basenji from the movie he made. I noticed that every time I'd see him he would be wearing a blue blazer and a tie — to walk his dog."

Muentz was a big fan of *Shane* ("I still think it's the greatest western ever made") but wasn't as impressed with *Blue Denim*, which at the time was in the midst of a publicity blitz. "Going to [the performing arts school], all of my friends were obsessed with the Actor's Studio, particularly James Dean, Marlon Brando, and Monty Clift. This was our fantasy. We would all go around imitating these guys and Brandon did not fit into that category, not with his blue blazer and conservative image."

One day, "I was holding my guitar and waiting for an elevator and he sees me and says, 'you play the guitar?' I said, 'Yeah,' and he said, 'Wow, would You show me something?

Hold on.' And he went to get his guitar and we sit on the stairs in the hallway and I start showing him a few things on the guitar. Next thing you know he's inviting me upstairs to his apartment to show him some more stuff."

"He took it really seriously," Muentz said about Brandon's guitar playing. "He took everything he did seriously. And he began to get pretty good." In a teen magazine article, Brandon mentioned Mike giving him lessons and said, "My favorite way to relax is to play the guitar. I practice for hours and practically wear my fingers to the bone. One time I had to stop because my fingers were bleeding."

Muentz had been hanging out in Greenwich Village for a couple of years, listening to the likes of Pete Seeger, Judy Collins, Tom Paxton and Dave Von Ronk in the coffeehouses, and on Sundays by the fountain in Washington Square Park. Muentz said he and a classmate (Janet Margolin, who a couple of years later would star in the movie *David and Lisa*) had a rare weekday permit to play guitar in this park.

Muentz showed Brandon around the village. He said it was fun because whereas going on his own or with other friends to the clubs, "I was lucky to get in the door, Brandon could walk into any place and instantly get recognized and treated like royalty."

"It's a very bizarre experience to be friends with a movie star and he was a movie star. You and I, we can go into any kind of retail store and the clerks will be polite to us, treat us nicely if they feel like it, in New York not necessarily, you buy your stuff and you leave. When I would walk into anyplace with Brandon the minute any one of the clerks or waitresses would spot him you would see the expression change on their face. It would like turn into a glow, and a smile, and it would be the classic, 'Do I know you, have I ever seen you before?' It would happen all the time. Instantly he would be treated like, 'Anything you want, anything, free dry-cleaning, free cigarettes'—it didn't matter."

He said that, "because of who Brandon was, the next thing you know we were meeting, and he was becoming close friends with, big guns in the folk scene, people like Fred Hellerman of The Weavers. We could walk into a little Greenwich Village club, and within seconds, 'Brandon deWilde? Oh yeah, man, I've heard of you,' and the next thing you know he's got famous musicians trying to get up close and personal with him because celebrities are drawn to their own. They liked being friends with a movie star and he liked being friends with recognized musicians."

Muentz said, "As I got [Brandon] more into the folk scene and hanging out in the village he was moving away from, 'Big name movie star goes to Hollywood but his real life is in the suburbs taking out the garbage and delivering the home newspaper.'"

When Brandon's friends from Baldwin visited him in the city Brandon would demonstrate his latest guitar-playing techniques and show them around the village. Rick Williams recalled "sitting in a corner" in a coffeehouse, "wearing sunglasses, thinking we were cool." He said, "Brandon got genuine respect from us as a musician where we were probably pretty aloof from his showbiz career."

Muentz said, "I was someone who lived downstairs who could tag along and party with him." After Muentz graduated from high school he got a job on Madison Avenue. "We would meet every day in this bar on 59th Street across from Bloomingdale's called Maggie's. He was always a really cool dresser. Anything he wore he looked really cool in. What would be considered preppy Ivy League clothes, he looked good in because he was a striking looking kid."

"He was a serious skirt chaser, serious, but he always liked to have a girlfriend. Saturday nights he always reserved for his date night. I would never see him Saturday. But the other six nights there was as good a chance as any we would do something. He would let me know in advance, he would grab his father's Oldsmobile and we would go cruising at eleven, twelve, one o'clock in the morning, chasing girls the same way you'd see in

American Graffiti but in a New York City setting.

"Anybody who looks at him, even if the girl was with a guy in a car, he started following them. All he wanted to do was see if the girl would be interested in jumping in his car. Then he wouldn't let them and we'd pull away. I used to get mad at him because sometimes we'd find a couple of really pretty girls."

Muentz said that from the period of *Blue Denim* through *Hud*, acting to Brandon "was a job. Everything was what he was going to be paid for a movie. He was not interested in the craft because he had been a working actor since *Member of the Wedding*. That's all he knew."

At eighteen, with a spate of TV guest appearances lined up, Brandon rented an apartment in West Hollywood for a year. "I birddog all the girls. I date everything," he told a reporter. A few months later he said, "I've dated enough girls to know I'm not interested in any girl in my business. They're only interested in my name and they're overly ambitious."

In California, he starred in an episode of the series *Thriller*, hosted by Boris Karloff and taped his second episode of *Wagon Train*. In 1962 he filmed an episode of *The Virginian*, the first ninety-minute TV Western. And he starred in two movies, *All Fall Down* and *Hud*.

Like his father, Brandon had signed up with the army under the RFA plan, and part of the deal was a six-month stint on a base. He was sent to Fort Dix in New Jersey and, not wanting to be singled out, enlisted under his family first name, Andre.

The second day at base, he reported to reception. A call had come from Paramount saying he was needed back in Hollywood for some voice dubbing for *Hud*. "Well, were they impressed," Brandon told Earl Wilson, columnist for the *New York Post*, on June 9, 1963. "The colonel put me on the bus himself. I'm in the army two days and I get a [temporary] pass."

Brandon said about his experience in the army, "I made a lot of friends, and I made a lot of enemies. I was treated like a normal human being, and that surprised me because you know how it is. There are always some guys who want to take a poke at you because you work in the movies."

While still in the army, Brandon was given another leave to film some scenes for a Walt Disney movie, *Those Calloways*. (Michael Muentz said, "It blew my mind that Walt Disney had more power than the military.") Brandon told Earl Wilson, "I have the lead. I'm playing myself, not somebody's nephew or brother." His character was Buck, who, with his trapper father played by Brian Keith, provides a sanctuary for the great flocks of migrating wild geese around their Vermont home.

Fritz, called a "strict disciplinarian" by a childhood friend of Brandon's, told a reporter, "Raising a professional child is much more difficult than bringing up other youngsters. Much as you try to keep them from being different you come to realize they are different. There are more tensions and problems."

John Anderson said, "Fritz talked a lot about problems with him. He wanted him to keep out of trouble, and Brandon was very headstrong. The only way he could discipline him was to take his driving license away."

Michael Muentz called Fritz, "a real weird duck. A captain in the army. Cold, but not un-nice. Bit of a drinker. It fueled Brandon's feeling that, 'Hey, he does it, I can drink too' so Brandon did quite a bit of drinking. He'd have fights with [his father in their apartment] you could hear two flights down. The next thing you know (Brandon)'d be ringing the bell and he'd want to talk about the fight with my mother."

Brandon said in *The Player* that during *Jamie*, "I began to hate rehearsing at home with my father. I liked rehearsing in the theater but when I was home I liked to go outside and play with the kids. I had terrible battles with my father. They would usually wind up with my calling him stupid and his calling me stupid—the way a lot of kids and their fathers yell at each other. We did that until I was about fifteen."

"My father is my personal, personal, personal manager," Brandon told the *Sunday News* in June of 1963. "We have a strange relationship. We fight constantly about everything. I guess it's because we're so close. If we were any closer, I'd be on the other side.

"The main thing we fight about is that for fifteen years my father has been trying to save my money."

From age twelve to seventeen, Brandon earned at least one hundred thousand dollars a year. At eighteen, he was the highest-paid actor his age. Rick Williams said, "there were times when I was in college when we would go into the city and he would pull out fifty bucks. I couldn't keep up that pace." Brandon's friends didn't know the wad he carried around was accumulated twenty-five-dollar weekly allowances and that his whole salary was funneled, sight unseen, into his trust fund. Brandon told a reporter he actually had more cash when he wasn't working because his father let him keep the weekly forty-dollar unemployment checks.

"My father and mother keep asking me what other American boy gets $25 a week allowance and I keep telling them that I'm not an average American boy," he told *Seventeen* in 1962. "If I go on a couple of dates during the week with a girl, $25 doesn't last any time at all. My folks are worried about my blowing all my money. I suppose I might blow it all. I don't have much of a head for money. That's one of my problems. I don't know how to handle things. I haven't had any experience. But I want to find out. That's one of the reasons I want to move out and do things for myself."

School was another source of tension and as far back as elementary school he met with a child psychologist to try and uncover the source of his deep antipathy to it. Now, Brandon didn't even want to think about going further than high school, telling a reporter, "I've never wanted to do anything but act and direct anyway. I think I'll be better off continuing to work instead of trying for a college degree."

Bruce Laffey said that at a party at the deWilde home around this time, "I was going through a terrible period, between shows, and really flat broke. It was a rainy night and I was thinking, 'I don't even have cab fare to get home.' Brandon and his father had been having a big talk inside about his plans, and just then they stepped out on the terrace, and Brandon said, 'Bruce, did you go to college?' I said 'no.' And he looked at Fritz and said, 'See! You don't have to go to college to be a success.'"

On Thanksgiving Day, 1963, Brandon was in Hollywood and Fritz was at work on Broadway, overseeing a matinee of *A Man for All Seasons*. So Genie spent the holiday at the home of Henry Moritz, a friend of the deWildes from their Walgreens out-of-work-actor days. Janet Hill remembered Genie "talk, talk, talking endlessly about Brandon. He seemed to be the only thing she was interested in."

9

All grown up

"Ten years ago, when I was a little boy, I made *Shane*," Brandon told a reporter. "I've made seven movies since then, but that's the picture everyone remembers me from. People still quote the line 'Come back Shane.' It follows me everywhere."

He reiterated a previous public complaint about not being allowed to stretch as an actor: "I'm always being offered parts as the good all-American boy. I suppose I have that kind of face. But I like to play parts with a little more depth. I'd prefer to play a kind of nut, with a kind of nastiness and meanness in him, rather than the boy next door who gets into a little trouble and then gets out of that little trouble."

In 1961, Brandon played a boy who couldn't tell fact from fantasy in "The Sorcerer's Apprentice," an episode of *Alfred Hitchcock Presents* set in a carnival. The finale was deemed too gruesome by the network, and it never aired. "I played a homicidal maniac, and it was too strong," he told a reporter for the *New York World Telegram* in May, 1963. "I enjoyed doing that, but I never get the chance. I'm always the good, decent boy."

And yet, he had made the transition from young boy to young man with an unbroken chain of A-list productions and with the golden aura that had enrobed him since he started in show business two-thirds of his life earlier as bright as ever. These were rare accomplishments for a child star.

He was playing an older Joey Starrett in both *All Fall Down* and *Hud*, but the movies were contemporary and high-powered enough to push Brandon into leading man territory.

All Fall Down was adapted from a 1960 novel by James Leo Herlihy, who had written the play of *Blue Denim* and who would publish the novel *Midnight Cowboy* in 1965. William Inge, whose scripts after *Come Back Little Sheba* included *Bus Stop* and *Splendor in the Grass*, wrote the screenplay. John Houseman produced the MGM movie and the director was John Frankenheimer, whose next project was *Manchurian Candidate* with Frank Sinatra.

Although Brandon's name is the fifth to appear in the opening credits, his character is the narrator and, as in *Shane*, his is the first and last face seen on the screen.

Brandon played sixteen-year-old Clinton, who worships his older brother Berry-Berry, a charming, immoral cad played by Warren Beatty. Clinton also adores the sensitive and beautiful Echo, played by Eva Marie Saint, who was in the pilot of *Jamie*. Echo falls in love with Berry-Berry, and Clinton gives his blessing to the relationship, which ends tragically for Echo. "You really do hate life," Clinton tells his brother in the last scene. "When you told me that before, I went along with you because I wanted to be just like you in every way I could. But I like life, Berry-Berry. So long, Berry-Berry."

Beatty was five years older than Brandon and a year earlier, on the heels of *Splendor in the Grass*, was proclaimed in *LIFE* as "a young man who is the most exciting American male in movies." In one poster for *All Fall Down*, Brandon's face was in a small corner square and Beatty's took up the rest. The headline read, "Male enough to attract a dozen women—not man enough to be faithful to one!"

But Brandon was not a fan. In *The Player*, he said, "One of the actors kept the script in his hand up until the last day and annoyed everyone else. It's difficult to act with someone who just sits and reads during rehearsals and is probably thinking he'll save the work until later." Bruce Laffey said Brandon named names in private. "Brandon was a very simple, together kind of a guy. He didn't like the cue cards and petulance. He just felt Warren was a cry-baby—'gimme this,' 'gimme that.' He didn't understand that."

Brandon had a happier experience with the director, telling a reporter that Frankenheimer was his favorite so far. A two-week rehearsal period before filming made the project feel like a play. And the director had a great set-side manner. "All he ever said to me before a scene was . . . well, first he'd take me over to a corner away from everyone, drop an arm around my shoulder, and say, 'Listen kid, just get in there and #$@ the %*& out of that @$% scene.' We really got along great. He's a swell guy."

Brandon said in *The Player* that *All Fall Down* "was the first time my father hadn't helped me with a role. I read the book the movie was based on four times, and felt I understood all the other characters as well as my own. I got so wound up at one point in the movie—while I was telling my brother what a bum he was— that I forgot that I was really just acting. I played a 16-year-old but I felt bigger and older than I'd ever felt before. It may be because I really felt I was playing somebody apart from myself, for the very first time. I could *play* a 16-year-old rather than *be* a 16-year-old.

"When my father saw the picture he said my performance was great. He's only given me about twelve compliments in my whole life so that meant a lot to me."

Newsweek positioned the movie in between the comic *You Can't Take it With You* and tragic *Long Day's Journey Into Night*, calling the direction "incisive," the message "striking," and the cast "almost miraculously sure. Colorful characters often tend to be loud and fade quickly; the color in *All Fall Down* is quiet and fast."

In *Hud*, the older person that Brandon (Lon) adores is his

uncle, the title character played by Paul Newman. It is the abuse of Lon's kind housekeeper (played by Patricia Neal) that opens his eyes to his hero's true character.

Paul Newman, sixteen years older than Brandon, told the author in a telephone interview in 1989 from his home in Connecticut that he helped cast the role of Lon. [The director Martin Ritt] said, 'how about Brandon deWilde?' and I said 'Wonderful!' We looked a lot alike. He looked a lot like my younger pictures, actually."

Hud and Lon pal around for much of the movie, hitting the bars after sundown. Patricia Neal said in a letter to the author dated December 2, 1988, that during the five weeks of filming in the dusty Texas town, the actors playing the characters did the same thing. "He and dear Paul Newman stayed in character off the set, as well as on. I think that Paul did it to help Brandon develop his character further. They had a very good time." Paul Newman recalled Brandon as "fun in front of the camera and he was good fun to have around."

Paul Newman bristled at the sanitization of his previous movie, an adaptation of Tennessee Williams's *Sweet Bird of Youth*, and he and the director were determined not to let that happen with *Hud*. Audiences and critics appreciated the result. *TIME* said the movie was a "shock for audiences who have been conditioned like laboratory mice to expect the customary bad-guy-is-really-good-guy reward in the last reel of a western."

Paul Newman called Brandon's portrayal of Lon, "terrific." Julie Harris thought it was Brandon's best role yet. Lou Peterson said, "I thought *Hud* was quite a remarkable performance. Brandon was going to be a very good actor. There's a split in most child actors. Some simply don't make it into adulthood. It's one of the problems. Margaret O'Brien didn't make it. But Brandon was doing that. *Hud* was the beginning of that route."

"By the time I'm twenty-five I want to be a director as well as act," an enthusiastic Brandon told a reporter. "I want to use the ideas that keep spurting out of me."

He continued, "I love the theater and want to do another play. It's still my true love. But movies and television are also fine, as long as I can be acting. I haven't done a lot of things other kids get to do— I've gone to only three or four dances in my life— but I'm not sorry. I'd never want to give up acting."

It didn't seem as though he would have to. A reporter for the *New Haven Register* wrote, "For a long while Brandon deWilde was just the little boy with the wondering face behind the horn-rimmed glasses. But he has certainly grown up, and the role of leading man is certainly on its way."

America's premier gossip columnist, Sheilah Graham, wrote in the *New York Mirror* on June 9, 1963, "I predict Brandon De Wilde will be one of our major stars."

10

There goes the movie star

In the December of 1963, the *New York Daily News* trumpeted "Our Little Brandon is All But Wed," reporting that the former child star of *The Member of the Wedding* was costarring in a real wedding, Brandon and debutante Susan Margot Maw having applied for their marriage license at City Hall. They had been engaged for six months.

Susan, said Bruce Laffey, "was divine. But everybody felt Brandon was a little young. 'Don't get married until you're thirty-five years old. Go out and live a bit.'"

Susan was three years younger than Brandon, with blond, Laura Petrie-styled hair. Her father Carlyle E. Maw was a prominent lawyer (and future advisor to Henry Kissinger) and she was a student at the Brearley school for girls on the upper East side. The *New York Daily News* reported that Susan made her society debut at the Debutante Ball in the Plaza Hotel, but would miss her next two coming-out balls because of her honeymoon.

Michael Muentz said that Brandon met Susan, "because of [Genie's] obsession with him being connected with the social register and dating girls and having friends that were in this high society in the east side of New York." He said of the couple,

"They were twins. She, too, was an Aries, blond, blue-eyed. They looked more like sister and brother than boyfriend and girlfriend. Both noses were stuck up in the air as far as you could go."

Early in their relationship, with Susan still in high school, Muentz said, "The Chad Mitchell Trio was playing Columbia University in the middle of the school week and he said, 'Hey, I need a chaperone to go with us because she's 17-years-old.' We were hanging out with the Trio backstage and next thing you know Susan says, 'school night, I got to get home' and Brandon had this expression, he was really pissed off."

Brandon told a magazine reporter, "She's going to be a great help to me. Especially as far as money goes—she's richer than I am." He told another reporter, "Susan has already taught me so much. She has increased my reading habit 100 percent." And, "She's the only girl I brought home that my parents really love."

Julie Harris said that during her Broadway run of *A Shot in the Dark* with Walter Matthau, "Someone knocked on the dressing room door. I said, 'Who is it?' And I heard, in a very deep voice 'Brandon.' Because he was all grown up. Susan was adorable. He was tall and blond and adorable-looking. They looked just like a prince and princess."

Brandon and Susan were married on December 19, 1963.

Greg Murphy recalled three days of parties preceding the ceremony at St. Bartholomew's Church at Park Avenue and Fiftieth Street in Manhattan. According to the *New York Herald Tribune*, Susan wore an ivory peau de soie empire-style gown embroidered with tiny pearls, and her tulle veil was attached to a coronet of heirloom lace borrowed from her mother. Greg Murphy and Rick Williams joined Susan's two brothers as ushers.

Michael Muentz said he and his mother (his father was deceased) were invited to the wedding reception but not the marriage ceremony.

Muentz said, "Nobody was involved in that wedding who

was part of Brandon's new world. No music friends, no hangers-on, nobody. Out of nowhere pops this high society character and the next thing you know he's his best man. About six months or so after the wedding he disappeared as fast as he came in."

The reception was at the private River Club in New York City. Guests included Beatrice Lillie and Rex Harrison.

Brandon and Susan had planned a three-week tour of Egypt and Greece. But on November 22, a month before their wedding, John F. Kennedy was assassinated. So for their honeymoon, the couple rode a train to Washington, DC instead. "It was the end of the mourning period for President Kennedy and we wanted to visit his grave," Brandon told a reporter.

During lunch with J. Edgar Hoover on the trip, the FBI director related to the couple how his agency had cracked the kidnapping case of Frank Sinatra Jr.

Also around this time, Brandon's animosity toward his father for pulling the purse strings so tightly when he was growing up vanished as he took control of a half-million-dollar trust fund. "I'm the only star I know who hasn't been robbed blind by his parents," he told reporters.

In the beginning of 1964, rumors circulated that Brandon would be nominated for another Best Supporting Actor Academy Award, this time for his role in *Hud*. He ended up being the only one of the movie's four leads in that movie not to be nominated. He did get to walk onto the stage at the Santa Monica Civic Auditorium to accept for the absent winner in his category, Melvyn Douglas, who had portrayed Brandon's grandfather. Handing the award to Brandon was Patty Duke who, the previous year at sixteen, had been the youngest person ever to win an Academy Award for best supporting actress, for *The Miracle Worker*.

Paul Newman told the author, "We made a big mistake with Hud. We gave him all the external graces—he was great with the ladies and attractive in that kind of macho way—but he was rotten to the core. We thought that young people would recognize that, but unfortunately they didn't. We created an involuntary anti-hero."

But this was no mistake for Newman, personally, because his seventeenth movie role turned him into Hollywood's hottest male star.

His luck was Brandon's misfortune. As when he had been paired with Warren Beatty in *All Fall Down*, Brandon couldn't help but be overshadowed. Further working against him for leading man traction, MGM bungled the marketing of *All Fall Down* so neither it, nor Brandon, even got much attention.

Stanley Kauffmann of *The New Republic* disliked Brandon's performance in *Hud*, writing, "His eyes are dead." But Louella Parsons graphed his career as still on the upswing, writing that his exclusion from the Oscars was because he had refused to lobby for it. "When he failed to make the charmed circle he indulged in neither beefs nor self-pity. I spent the evening of the day the nominations were announced with him, and his only comment was, 'Gosh, I'm the only one in the cast who didn't make it.' Then he changed the subject."

In February of 1964 he rented an apartment in Hollywood for a few months for work, taping an episode of a series hosted by Jack Palance called *The Greatest Show on Earth* and signing to appear in a three-part television miniseries called *The Tenderfoot* for *Walt Disney's Wonderful World of Color*. When Susan joined Brandon for their four-month wedding anniversary Brandon introduced her to Ethel Waters at the Pasadena Playhouse, where the actress was portraying Berenice.

"Everything's going for me now," Brandon told *Seventeen* in its May 1965 issue when he was twenty-three-years-old. "I was the first one cast for *In Harm's Way*—that's a terrific Otto Preminger movie about the Navy after Pearl Harbor—and I've got a good part, that of John Wayne's son. I'm appearing on Broadway this spring too in *A Race of Hairy Men!*, an exciting play about college students during school vacation. And I've been working on a record album . . . I've got four and a half Martin guitars now—

one's broken—and I've been practicing folk music and blues. I also made *Those Calloways*, a good dramatic picture for Disney. Why, I even fight a wolf. Barehanded!"

In Harm's Way reunited Brandon with Patricia Neal, who perhaps reflecting her Best Actress Oscar for *Hud*, had the higher billing.

Back in New York, Fritz was collaborating with Robert Whitehead and Elia Kazan on a repertory theater group in the newly constructed Lincoln Center. Brandon was excited about being invited to join the second two-year program. Actors were paid a fraction of Brandon's salary in movies and TV, but after working as an actor for fourteen years, he said, "I will finally have a chance to really learn something about my business."

Brandon and Susan were renting a five-room apartment on Eighty-Fourth Street. "We want to move to the Village," Susan said in a magazine article accompanied by a photo of her in a mini-skirt. "We go down there all the time. All our friends are in the folk world."

Brandon and Josh White Jr., a classmate from the Professional Children's School and son of the folk-blues guitarist and singer, spent evenings together trying to replicate the flashy finger-picking of Dick Rosmini, who was considered the best twelve-string guitar player in the world. "Brandon picked better than I did," said Josh. "It made me mad sometimes how good he was."

Susan and Brandon took classes together in psychology and philosophy at the New School in Greenwich Village. Brandon also studied Motion Pictures as Social and Personal Commentary and habitually brought his Super-8 movie camera along when visiting their white farmhouse on two hundred acres in the White River Junction area of Vermont.

Until now, Brandon's life as a child star had been painted in broad, bright strokes but in an interview with Louella Parsons he said he wouldn't put his own child into the business. "The more I think about it the more a good, solid, formal education without interruption is important. When I look back, of course I missed something. I grew up in a world of adults. I was not good at sports. There were times I wished I didn't have to study lines and could play baseball. Also I took a lot of ribbing from other kids —'There goes the movie star.'"

He told Louella Parsons' rival gossip columnist, Hedda Hopper, "I often wonder what would have happened if I hadn't been in this business. Sometimes I curse it. I [don't] know if I could do anything else if I was in a car accident and was terribly maimed. I'd like to do something else but I'm afraid to risk it."

It was around this time that Brandon signed with his first outside agency. Ed Robbins of William Morris said, "Fritz felt that Brandon could benefit from national and international representation by being with a major talent agency." He added, "It's one thing to have a parent-child relationship. But when one of the parents is also the business manager you feel they have a double hold on you. It gets a bit touchy— where does the parent take over and lose objectivity in making career decisions? You can't fault the parent the way you can an outside manager on the way your career is or isn't going."

A few months into the relationship, "Brandon wanted to deal directly with me and the lawyer. I would still stay in touch with Fritz as a courtesy to let him know what was going on, but in the actual negotiations, I would coordinate with Brandon and the attorney."

Robbins said "Fritz was very concerned about what Brandon did. What he wanted for Brandon was a very good, solid career. Everything Brandon had done in his career, plays or films starting with *Member of The Wedding*, was very distinguished. The caliber of projects that Fritz worked on when he went on his own were also very prestigious—producers, directors, writers were always first class. That's what we wanted for Brandon."

In the early months of 1965, Brandon guest-starred in an episode of *The Defenders*, put out by the prestigious duo behind *Twelve Angry Men*, writer Reginald Rose and actor E. G. Marshall.

Then he went straight into rehearsals for his first Broadway play in seven years and his first as an adult. He was the star.

Writer Evan Hunter had struck movie gold with *Blackboard Jungle* and *The Birds*. His play *A Race of Hairy Men!* is about a group of boys who borrow a New York apartment to meet their girlfriends. It had received critical acclaim during its London opening the previous summer, and even though it had closed in three weeks, Brandon liked it and so did his parents. Family friend Henry Moritz talked it up to their other friends, and many became investors.

The play fared the same as it had in London, opening at the Henry Miller Theater April 17, 1965 and closing before May. "We didn't make any money," said one of the investors John Gillespie, "but we did get free seats." *In Harm's Way* was greeted indifferently by the critics and public. *Those Calloways* also did only moderately well. Robert Whitehead pulled out of the Lincoln Center theater group Brandon had been so excited about joining.

And then came, said his manager Ed Robbins, "a very difficult time of finding meaningful roles for Brandon. I think it was a combination of things. There was a lack of roles and he wasn't that interested in pursuing roles."

Family friend Lyle Bettger said, "I personally felt that Brandon began to feel his career was slipping. This is only a gut feeling we had, the result of hearing bits and pieces of gossip and letters from Genie that hinted that all was not as well as it had been a few years earlier."

* * *

Brandon took after his father in many ways. Fritz dressed in the urbane manner of thirties film star William Powell. In the mid-sixties when fashions were considerably looser, Brandon explained to a reporter, "I want all my clothes to be in good taste. I like to dress up and wear a tie and jacket, or instead of the shirt and tie I'll wear a sport shirt." He apologized for showing up with his pants tucked into boots, saying, "I get a certain pride out of not looking like a slob but I didn't want to keep you waiting."

They both loved music. And while John Anderson said that Fritz, "in his fifties and sixties still looked like a kid," Brandon's age seemed suspended at sixteen, the age he convincingly played in *All Fall Down* when he was three years older. He complained to a reporter, "Only last week a cop stopped me at a red light and said, 'Pull over, kid, let me see your driving license.' It happens all the time."

Ed Robbins said, "People weren't writing for the teenage market." And anyway, "he was too old to be playing sixteen- and seventeen-year-olds. At a certain point you feel you want to move on and play more mature roles."

Tommy Rettig had a lot in common with Brandon; his early career had been as dazzling as Brandon's and he looked younger than his age. Rettig was thirteen in 1954 when he played one of TV's most enduring roles: Lassie's best friend. But he told me in an interview in his Marina del Rey apartment in 1992 that the TV show "was crap compared to what I had been doing." This included costarring with Marilyn Monroe, working with Otto Preminger and playing Dr. Seuss's alter ego in *5,000 Fingers of Dr. T.*

He made eighteen movies and in his last season as Jeff Miller on *Lassie* he was the highest-paid actor in Hollywood. "Everything just rolled," he said.

From about the age of eleven, "I didn't have to read for parts," he said. "Go in, sit down, talk with the director or producer for half an hour—'do you want to do it?' Later it was going in and, 'Let me entertain you.' That's terribly psychologically damaging."

When Rettig was eighteen, "work was non-existent. I spent my whole twenties very frustrated— typically what happens to kid actors. Biologically, you're supposed to, as late teenagers, be getting wins, coming up, getting accepted into the adult world, and that's natural. For someone who's been famous as a child and no longer is as an adult, you're on a skid going this way when all your friends are going that way.

"It's separating. It's like growing up as royalty. You're just different from the kid across the street, and when you're a kid, you don't want to be different. You want to be friends with the kid across the street. It's a form of child abuse that's not recognized. I don't know of any male child actor who let his own child get into the business. It's difficult for the industry because how do we create an art form that represents children in life without having child actors?"

Rettig had a number of well-publicized run-ins with the law pertaining to the possession of marijuana and cocaine, and he promoted a "personal growth seminar" on the benefits and self-management of recreational drugs. He was a computer entrepreneur and programmer when he died at fifty-four in 1996.

In 1964, Rick Williams had just graduated from St. Lawrence College and on a visit to LA he met up with Brandon.

"He was certainly doing more than I was, but I sensed he wasn't finding a lot of success as an actor. He was short, around 5'9". He wasn't going to replace John Wayne. There were a lot of tensions. Being on his own away from his parents, he was starting to encounter some of the real world.

"He was at a crossroads. Brandon got married years before the rest of us thought of getting married. All the rest of us went off to college. He didn't. That's where things drifted. He found himself in a position where he didn't have the education to do anything other than what he was doing. He had a name in acting, and he would make a fraction of the money doing anything else. I had the impression he was probably coming to some realization that as a long-term thing he would have a fairly rocky road as an actor. Here's a kid who skyrocketed as a child, *Shane* and all, and then it was tapering just when the rest of us were getting started with our lives."

11

Member of the band

In the spring of 1965 folk music was suddenly passé. Bob Dylan fused the genre with rock and the Beatles drew fifty-thousand screaming teens to Shea Stadium, while their compatriots hijacked the American rock charts with songs like "Satisfaction" and "Mrs. Brown, You've Got a Lovely Daughter."

Brandon told the *New York World Telegram* that he only watched his own movies and the Beatles' *A Hard Day's Night*. "It's the best movie ever made. I've seen it five times."

Josh White Jr. recalled this period for Brandon as "between things. He wasn't doing much of anything, no plays or movies. We'd drive together to some of my gigs in Albany or Buffalo. The two of us and our wives would hang out, play tunes together." He said that he and Brandon, "discovered marijuana and did it a lot."

Margaret Garland, Genie's friend from her single days in New York City, went on to co-star in the 1950s TV series *Tom Corbett's Space Cadet* and married son of *Oklahoma!* and *South Pacific* lyricist Oscar Hammerstein II. She remembered that when the talk turned to the rapidly changing times, Genie mentioned her own youth: "being on a bus with her mother and her mother saying, 'I won't go anyplace with you if you don't wipe off that

Joan Crawford mouth.'" Fritz was not as philosophical. "He was confused about the change over the whole country and Brandon changing from shy and preppy to having long hair and being interested in rock music."

Michael Muentz said, "The next thing you know he was friends with Ralph Scala and Ron Gilbert [vocalist/keyboardist and bassist respectively of the Blues Magoos, a folk group that evolved into one of the first psychedelic rock bands and is best known for its 1967, #5 hit "(We Ain't Got) Nothin' Yet"]. He developed a new circle of friends I knew nothing about."

Gram Parsons helped to pioneer country rock by melding country music with rock 'n roll, inspiring the likes of the Rolling Stones and the Eagles. In 1965, the charismatic rich kid from Florida was soaking up the vibrant folk music scene in Cambridge, Massachuestts with his latest backing band, The Like. The band featured Ian Dunlop on bass, John Nuese on guitar and Tom Snow on electric piano.

Gram was a fan of the Blues Magoos and it was at a show of theirs at the Café Wha that he and Brandon met.

Muentz said, "Gram was one of the most brilliant guys I ever heard. He had a way with words that was amazing. But so did Brandon. Brandon was incredibly quick-witted, sarcastic. They could finish each other's sentences and it was amazing just to watch these two guys talk. When Brandon wasn't putting you down or ranking you out or if he was aiming it at someone else he could be very funny. You would laugh at everything he said."

It was around this time that Brandon hung out with the Beatles in the Bahamas while they were making the movie *Help*. According to Joey Stec, Brandon's best friend from 1969, Brandon had been recruited as an acting advisor. "He returned with his musical aspirations to the sky and he said to Mickey [Gauvin, drummer in Gram's band], 'I want to get that guy Gram who comes in to see the Blues Magoos. I want to get everybody up here for like a two-week-long jam session.'"

Dunlop said, "We rehearsed some of the stuff in a studio

on four-track, which was pretty reasonable equipment for those days. Some of [Brandon's] songs were really nice. Unpretentious folk rock. One of the lines was 'I'll do my share so that you'll care.'" Brandon also recorded Buck Owens's "Together Again" and "Just as Long as You Love Me," Little Richard's "Rip it Up," and Wilson Pickett's "In the Midnight Hour." Buddy Lucas, a legendary session player best known as a tenor saxophonist, added harmonica.

Brandon arranged for the demo session, paying for it himself, in the hopes that it would get him a music agent and a recording contract.

Before long, the Like evolved to the International Submarine Band. John Nuese said the band spent a lot of time in Brandon's and Susan's apartment, recalling an octagonal room that let in a lot of light as "a perfect room to jam in." Nuese said that, "He was like family. We loved the guy."

Michael Muentz said of Brandon, "I didn't think he was that great a musician. Most actors aren't. All actors want to be musicians and all musicians want to be actors."

Jon Corneal, drummer in a second version of the Submarine Band, said, "When Brandon sang he sang straight to the point. He didn't try to sound like Elvis or someone else. He was not as good a guitar player but played pretty good rhythm guitar."

Ralph Scala said that in Brandon's apartment, as in the rambling house turned makeshift studio Gram was renting in the Bronx, "It was drugs, tape recorders, and instruments. We'd go for days making up songs, playing songs, then break to pass out, change clothes." Brandon kept his Tandberg tape recorder going, capturing musical accompaniment by hairbrushes, cereal boxes and shoes. He also taped many comic riffs by Pelbert J. Long and LuLu Round—alter egos of himself and Gram—touching on cultural references as disparate as Andy Warhol, Wild Bill Hickok, Carl Perkins and J. Edgar Hoover.

Brandon and Gram liked to harmonize, with Nuese comparing their sound to the Everly Brothers and saying that next to Emmylou Harris, "Gram's best duet singing was with Brandon."

According to Muentz, "Brandon loved to stay up all night and play music. That was his life. He never liked to be alone and he always wanted to play so he would find anyone who was willing to hang out with him and stay up all night and play bass guitar, rhythm guitar, whatever. Music began to form seventy-five percent of his life at this point and his acting career began to disappear."

Now, when Susan and Brandon went to Vermont, their musician friends went, too. Ian Dunlop said that during one of the stays the boys dropped acid, and Brandon filmed them spray-painting an old tractor with stripes and swirls in florescent pink, orange, and green.

Michael Muentz reconnected with Brandon in the fall of 1965. "He gets an apartment on 440 West End Avenue, invites me over and first thing I noticed is Susan is dressed like a little hippie girl 'cause it's 1965 and things are changing. There's another girl there too, with long brown hair, also very hippie-looking. I can't make any sense of that one but I'm not going to argue about it because Susan didn't seem to have an issue with it."

He was at Brandon's house in 1966 when, "The doorbell rings and in walks Gram Parsons with all this acid he brought down from Harvard that he got from Timothy Leary and next thing you know I'm taking my first acid trip. That was quite a night."

Muentz had just been drafted. "I already had one physical and the next physical I'd be on the bus. This is just when [President Lyndon] Johnson had escalated the war. The next thing you know Gram's telling me how he got out of the army being stoned out of his mind and and they were going to help me get out of the army the same way. So Brandon and Gram drove me out in my little Porsche to the draft board, me stoned on amphetamines, up for three days, and I got so freaked out because Brandon gave me a tab of acid just before I went to the draft board."

Jon Corneal first met Brandon in Los Angeles at a party. "It just so happened that *The Member of the Wedding* was playing on TV. He had those big glasses on. Right after that party, there was another one at Peter Fonda's house. Quite a number of big-time people were there. Of all of them, Brandon seemed to be the least affected, least of a quote, unquote 'star.' He always felt like real people. I'd lived in Nashville and had been around some country music stars but never around that many big-time actors. You'd always assume they might not be like other people. The first thing you noticed about Brandon was, here's this guy, a star, and he didn't act like one at all."

When Ian Dunlop met Brandon, he had seen him in one episode of *Wagon Train* in 1961, and "it didn't click that he was the actor." In his 2011 memoir *Breakfast in Nudie Suits*, he recounts that *Shane* played in a movie theater in New York City in 1966 and the Submarine Band went with Brandon to watch it. The first re-release had been in 1959 and this time the publicity campaign proclaimed, "It's back: the greatest Western of them all."

Ron Gilbert, Blues Magoos bassist, said that Brandon "reminded me of a bio I read of Clark Gable. [Gable] didn't like to hang out with movie people and neither did Brandon. Brandon loved music. He liked to jam. He loved to do what I loved to do—sit and listen to records. He liked B.B. King, Sam and Dave, Dyke & The Blazers, Otis Redding. Movies didn't come up. The subject made him uncomfortable. If I introduced him by his full name he would say, 'Hi. My name is Brandon. What do you want to play?'"

Ralph Scala: *Everyone in the acting world was so straight. He became alienated with the group that was feeding him.*

Dick Rosmini: *I was surprised that he hung out with the Gram Parsons crowd. They were a little too fast for my taste.*

Josh White Jr.: *Everyone has limits to what he will experiment with. When he started to experiment with LSD we drifted apart.*

* * *

Peppy Castro of the Blues Magoos: *The music scene really started to blow up big time around then. Hendrix, the Beatles, and all the cult figures, were coming out of music. Acting didn't do it for him. It was like going into the office. Music was a lot more exciting. It gave him peace. Brandon was fighting Brandon, and we were people having fun.*

Ian Dunlop: *The contact of theater isn't found in TV or movies. That's why gigging with bands appealed to him. It's the same format of playing to an audience in a hall.*

Dick Rosmini: *Music was Brandon's idea. Regardless of how talented he was in it, it wasn't Fritz's idea, and that was a big plus.*

Norman Gimbel, half of the duo Gimbel and Fox, was one of the most prolific pop lyricists of the 1970s, writing such standards as "The Girl from Ipanema" and "Killing Me Softly". In a letter dated January 12, 1990, he wrote to the author: *I'm not sure how the meeting between Brandon and myself came about, that is, who actually arranged it. Though I'm sure it was by a mutual friend. We met once or twice, I think, in the family apartment in Manhattan.*

Brandon was interested in cutting a record and I was an up-and-coming lyricist. The purpose of the meeting, for me at least, was to audition his voice. I found it rather pleasant. He sang and played guitar in what you might call the folk idiom. I probably suggested he take lessons on guitar if he wanted to sing and accompany himself.

The so-called 'folk music' was in vogue at that time and many singers could make their way in the music business with nice pleasant musical voices. The very 'unslick' quality of folk type singing made the artist more natural and accessible to the young people. His nice vocal talent, his film work, and his strong desire to sing, I believed could possibly make the project work and give him a chance at a recording deal. I imagined my function in the arrangement would be to write the songs.

I later learned that he wanted to write his own songs. I didn't wish to function on the project as the entrepreneur so I lost interest.

Dick Rosmini: *I was working with other actors. The whole Bonanza bunch for one. They found they could make very large money by appearing at rodeos. They would come out, sing three songs. It was very difficult for [Dan, who played 'Hoss' in the TV series] Blocker to count to 10 as a musician* and I would make them look perfectly reasonable.

    Brandon called me up. Fritz came to one recording session. I was preventing him from being visible because he made Brandon nervous. I made him sit in the hallway. He was perfectly charming about it. We wound up doing about half a dozen cuts. What I recorded and what I did with him were completely different. He did quasi-folk with electric guitar. He was not commercially presentable without a lot more work. He didn't have a musical point of view. He didn't play very well. He was fair. He was working on it but not with any real pressure. He was very much interested in music, so who knows? If someone had cooked him up a nice big steak, he would have eaten it.

    Ian Dunlop said this session had a very different feel from the earlier, freewheeling one with members of his band. "We recorded some really rather contrived and nervous music. There was an attitude in those days—If someone is washed up in something what do you do? Repackage them for country and western, sort of like they tried to do with Ricky Nelson. All sorts of people got repackaged for the mom-and-pop Ohio market. That was a real brainstorm someone had. We cut the song 'Together Again' like a waltz ballad. There have been some very moving and heartrending versions of that song but that isn't what Brandon should have been doing. He was in his early twenties. He should have been more toward pop. If someone had a bit of brains, he would have put him in that genre. In 1966, it was a whole new thing happening, and he was a pretty photogenic guy.

    "I think his management figured, 'Well, we tried it with you and it didn't work. We want you to put that idea out of your head.'"

Photo Gallery #2

A radio interview with Maggi McNellis, hostess of "Celebrity Talks" and "one of the ten best-dressed women in America" in the late 1950s.

Brandon returned to Broadway after a five-year hiatus in 1958's *Comes a Day*.

PICCIOTTI'S
Restaurant
4th and Du Pont Streets — Phone OL 5-6471

THE CAST
(In order of appearance)

C. D. Lawton	BRANDON de WILDE
Joe Glover	MICHAEL J. POLLARD
Caroline Lawton	DIANA van der VLIS
Isabel Lawton	JUDITH ANDERSON
Katherine Eubanks	RUTH HAMMOND
Tydings Glenn	GEORGE C. SCOTT
Charley Lawton	ARTHUR O'CONNELL
Jim Culpepper	LARRY HAGMAN
Gordie Eubanks	CHARLES WHITE
Lorraine Glenn	EILEEN RYAN
Bud, a Mexican	JOHN DUTRA

*Clothes for Town and Country
for the most Gala Occasion*

Jo Robinson Inc.
911 Washington St.

Parking in the rear while shopping at . . .

11

He likes show tunes and Johnny Mathis best, but rock 'n roll records are eating into his allowance, informed the cover story with the headline "Brandon Blasts Off" and the subhead, "deWilde's in orbit, shooting skyward." Brandon explained in the article that the trademark, teardrop scar next to his eye was a "plain old birthmark" coming from a forceps delivery.

Carol Lynley was Brandon's first off-screen and on-screen girlfriend.

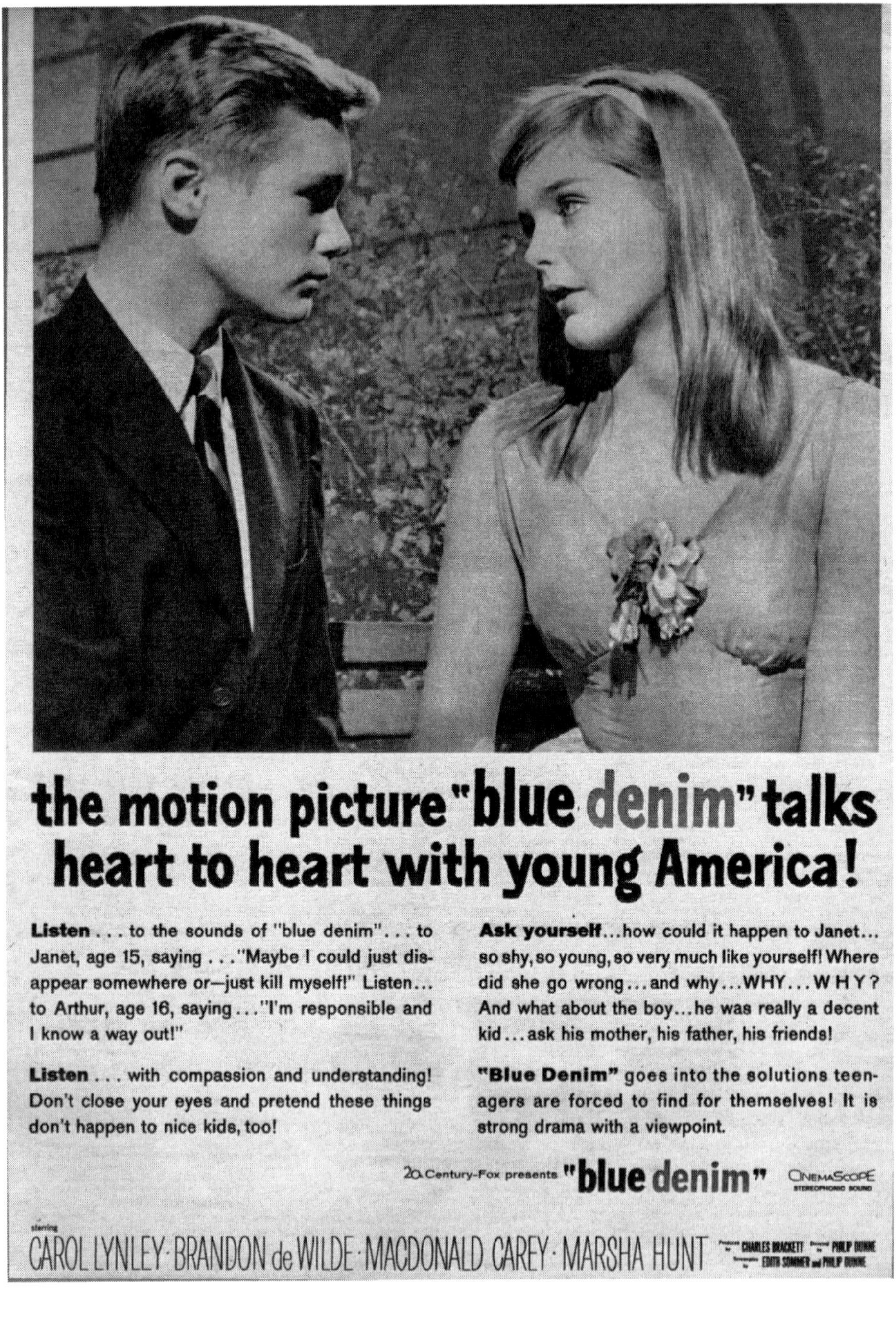

the motion picture "blue denim" talks heart to heart with young America!
Listen . . . to the sounds of "blue denim" . . . to Janet, age 15, saying . . . "Maybe I could just disappear somewhere or—just kill myself!" Listen . . . to Arthur, age 16, saying . . . "I'm responsible and I know a way out!"
Listen . . . with compassion and understanding! Don't close your eyes and pretend these things don't happen to nice kids, too!
Ask yourself...how could it happen to Janet... so shy, so young, so very much like yourself! Where did she go wrong . . . and why . . . WHY . . . W H Y ? And what about the boy...he was really a decent kid . . . ask his mother, his father, his friends!
"Blue Denim" goes into the solutions teenagers are forced to find for themselves! It is strong drama with a viewpoint.
20 Century-Fox presents "blue denim"
CINEMASCOPE
STEREOPHONIC SOUND
starring
CAROL LYNLEY · BRANDON de WILDE · MACDONALD CAREY · MARSHA HUNT
CHARLES BRACKETT PHILIP DUNNE
EDITH SOMMER and PHILIP DUNNE

A still from the movie *All Fall Down* that mirrored real life for Brandon. "He got genuine respect from us as a musician," said a childhood friend, "where we were probably pretty aloof from his showbiz career."

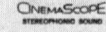

A scene from *Blue Denim*

Brandon with Paul Newman and Melvyn Douglas in *Hud*.

Paul Newman said that Brandon looked just like a younger version of himself.

Brandon's parents were still his agents here and he said in 1961, "All three of us discuss every part that's sent to us."

The chauffeur helps with Susan Margot Maw's veil following the wedding ceremony.

A press photo of the newlyweds.

Brandon and his family had high hopes for this 1965 Broadway show that was by the writer of *Blackboard Jungle* and *The Birds*.

Those Calloways, with Linda Evans.

Brandon came out of acting retirement after receiving bad news from his accountant. On left, he appears in *Love American Style*, and below in *The Virginian*.

Brandon was reunited with Julie Harris, who played his girlfriend's mother, in a TV episode where he played a teenage serial killer.

Brandon, at his ranch house in the San Fernando Valley, a few weeks before he met his second wife. *Collection of Michael Muentz.*

Come along for the ride, Baby--
You're gonna love it!
Josh has the plane and the H-Bomb and he's gonna blow Ft. Knox higher than you've ever been. The President's puckered, Gen. Gobohare's golf game is ruined and Col. Reason has turned queer as a three dollar bill.
So press the button, Baby--It'll be...
WILD IN THE SKY
SECURITY FAULT
WARHEAD ALARM
An American International Release
© 1972 American International Pictures, Inc.

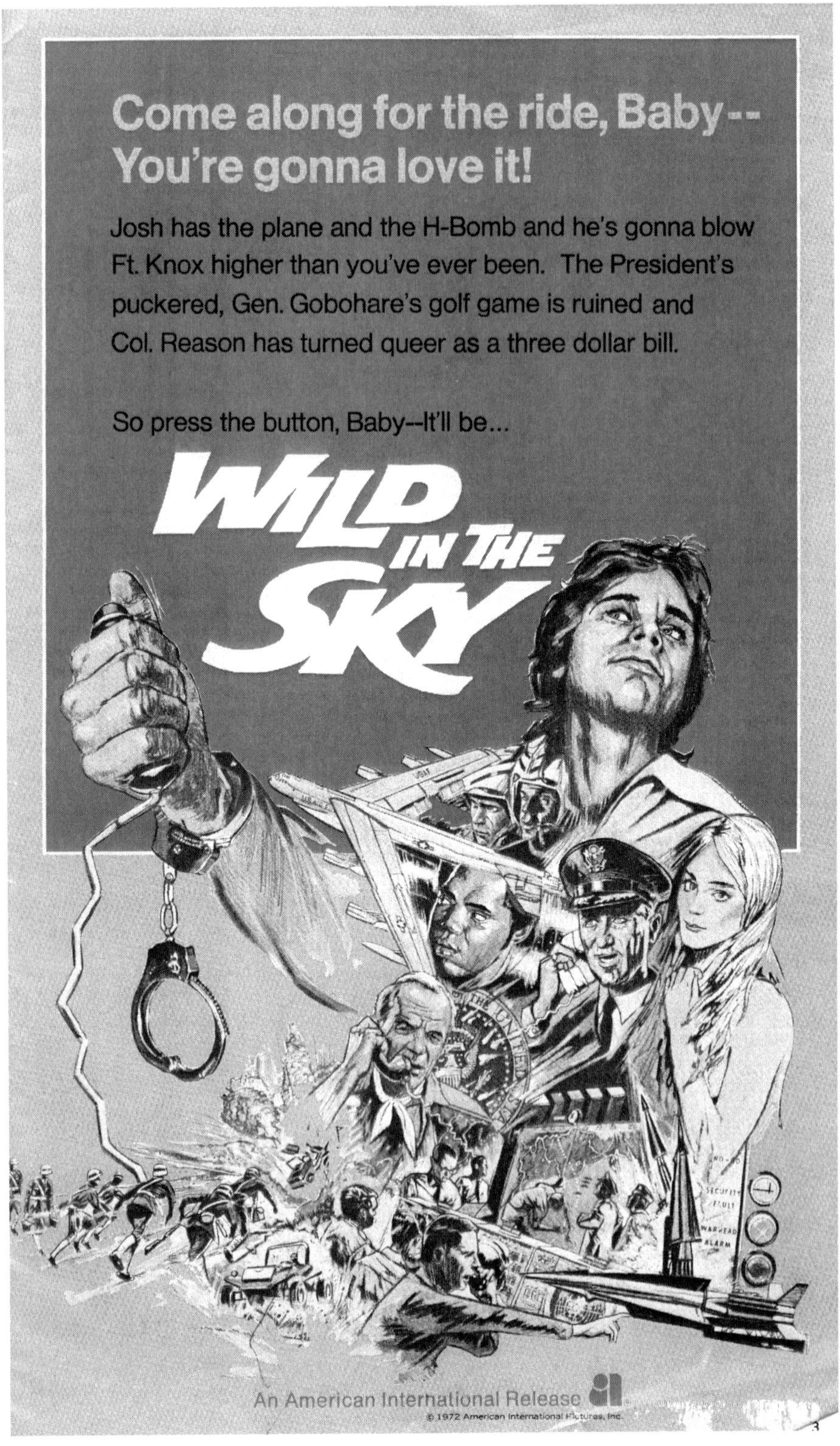

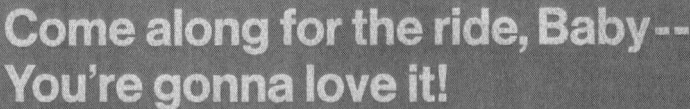

Brandon and Janice, with his son Jesse by his first wife Susan. Brandon and Susan shared custody.

"It was my first marriage," said Janice, "and Brandon found a dressmaker to make my wedding dress out of a sketch that I made."

The Elitch Theatre Company

Helen G. Bonfils — Producer
Whitfield Connor — Executive Administrator

81st Anniversary Season

MAUREEN O'SULLIVAN
and
BRANDON DE WILDE

in

"BUTTERFLIES ARE FREE"

Monday, June 19 through Saturday, July 1
Evening performances at 8:30 p.m.
Wednesday and Saturday matinees at 2:15 p.m.

NEXT ATTRACTION

MICKEY ROONEY
in the howling farce
"SEE HOW THEY RUN"
Monday, July 3
for Two Weeks

"He was insecure about his acting," said Janice about Brandon during rehearsals for *Butterflies are Free*. "He would ask me, 'do I look like I'm blind?'"

One of the last photos of Brandon. "He just looked so beautiful," said Janice. "A twinkle in his eye and a big ol' smile on his face. He was getting healthy, putting some weight back."

UPI Photo by Joe Marquette.

DE WILDE, BRANDON (NOT SHOWN) WRECKAGE OF CAMPER

JUL 7 1972

'72 JUL 7 AM 11:05

Employees at Rapid Towing yard 11805½ W. Colfax examine wreck of Camper Van driven by

RRV 52709

DE WILDE CAMPER VAN IS CRUMPLED MASS

UPI Photo by Joe Marquette

Employes of Rapid Towing yard, 11805½ W. Colfax Ave., Lakewood, examine the wreckage of the camper van which was driven by actor Brandon de Wilde Thursday afternoon when it struck a guardrail then caromed into a flatbed truck on W. 6th Ave. near Kipling St. De Wilde, best known for his role as a boy in the classic Western film "Shane" died at St. Anthony Hospital at 7:30 p from injuries suffered in mishap. (SEE STORY ON P5x

Photo by Joe Marquette

Fatal 4x5¼ Fri P|x HOME Refer to P.3

12

So you wanna be a rock 'n roll star

The lead paragraph of an *L.A. Times* feature article read, "Shane, Shane, come back Shane! It's been 17 years since he started acting and in that time he's done a lot of TV, motion pictures and stage work, but in the minds of many he's still remembered best as a kid."

In the spring of 1966, Brandon appeared as a frightened army private in an episode of *Combat* with Vic Morrow called "Sudden Terror" and onstage in a small Los Angeles theater in *Tom Jones*.

"For the movie business, he maintained a front," said Ron Gilbert. "He never worked stoned. If he had a gig, he would be straight for several days."

In the fall he was in *The Confession*, an hour-long drama about a young boy and his fiancée agreeing on a suicide pact — she dies, he doesn't. A police officer, played by Arthur Kennedy, is convinced Brandon's character is guilty of murder.

This episode was part of *ABC Stage 67*, a short-lived series that—harkening back to the 1950s — brought culture to the masses. But it was still TV, and Jon Corneal said that, "People were a bit snooty" about that medium then. "It wasn't hip.

Brandon wasn't getting the class parts he was getting in his childhood."

According to Bruce Laffey, "Fritz would say, 'I can't get Brandon a job because he won't cut his hair'— then it was guitars. Fritz complained a lot about that. Fritz was just worried about his future." "I've gotten a few rhubarbs because of it being this length," Brandon told an *LA Times* reporter about his hair, "but I think people should wear [it] the way they want to and it's nobody's business."

Lou Peterson said, "Genie was very concerned about Brandon, exceedingly so. She would call me and ask if I knew anyone who was casting. She would simply say that Brandon needs work."

Ian Dunlop said, "He started refusing work. It was obvious why. Everyone always thought of *Shane*. 'What's that little kid doing driving an Oldsmobile? He shouldn't be allowed to drive.' People would recognize the name, then see a man in front of them in a mod corduroy jacket smoking an Old Gold, not a bright-eyed Huckleberry Finn. I know he went through this a lot."

Ed Robbins, Brandon's manager at the time, said, "If you want to keep working, you sometimes just take what comes along. You can't afford financially to keep saying no, and it's also important that you have a film out there so people in the industry know at least you're working, that somebody wants you. But Brandon wanted it on his terms, and he did say no."

Michael Muentz said, "His ego was in the clouds, 'they got to come to me,' and eventually nobody came to him. He was beyond ambition. He never had ambition. It was just handed to him. He never had to audition for anything. That's very heady stuff, when you don't have to audition."

Dunlop said that Brandon's management "encouraged him to move out to Hollywood and try to get work there because it just wasn't happening in New York for him."

This was in 1967. He did move to the west coast but was absent from TV for two years, from movie theaters for three, and never again appeared on Broadway.

* * *

They called him 'the kid' until he was 24 years old. It was 'put the spot on the kid' or 'Okay, we're ready for the kid.' It got a little tiresome for a fellow who had been shaving for six years.

So one day Brandon deWilde called up his agent and told him the heck with it. He didn't want to work anymore.

'Man, the storm that caused. My agent blew his mind and told me I was crazy,' recalls a much older twenty-seven-year-old deWilde. 'But when I made the decision to quit I felt there was a stagnancy quality creeping into all of my performances. I was always playing someone's younger brother or a very moody young man with something brooding inside that you didn't find out about until the end of the picture. It's hard to describe the lack of identity that I felt between the ages of 13 and 22. I worked fairly regularly and in some good films. But I knew absolutely nothing about myself.' Newspaper interview with Nadine M. Edwards, 1970.

Bruce Laffey said that when Brandon made the decision to quit acting in late 1966, "His family was in shock. Brandon was very close to his mother and father. It didn't seem like him to suddenly branch out [into music]. He was serious about being an actor. Why do you do things that have nothing to do with your profession? The way Fritz told it, it had a lot to do with Susan, her friends and all of that. He felt that influence came from the married side of his life."

Ed Robbins said, "He had always played very proper young men. Maybe music gave him the opportunity to kick up his heels."

* * *

Brandon bought a house in Topanga Canyon from Bob Denver, of *Dobie Gillis* and *Gilligan's Island* fame. The house was nestled in a ravine, on a mountain up a long, curvy road. In

1967, Susan gave birth to their son, Jesse. Brandon called him Jerd.

Brandon looked up a castmate in 1958's *Comes a Day* and *In Harm's Way* who was the son of the Broadway musical theater legend Mary Martin. With his starring role in *I Dream of Jeannie*, Larry Hagman was now being watched by more people every week than had watched his mother in her entire career.

Brandon and Larry Hagman had gotten stoned together on the set of *In Harm's Way* but now Brandon had even more in common with another scion of entertainment royalty living in Los Angeles, Peter Fonda. The only son of Henry Fonda started his career as a mainstream actor in an episode of the TV show *The New Breed* with Patty McCormack and as the love interest of Sandra Dee in the film *Tammy and the Doctor*, played his guitar constantly, and wanted to record an album.

Brandon joined Fonda on the set of a psychedelic movie *The Trip*, directed by Roger Corman, and appears fleetingly in a bar scene. "We've just finished making a movie," intones Peter Fonda in the trailer, "dealing with the most talked-about subject of the day: LSD. " A woman's voice purrs, "The wildest of pleasures possess you," and a man's deep voice has the last word: "It will blow your mind."

Philip Proctor was a member of the cult comedy quartet Firesign Theater, and more recently voiced characters in such Pixar films as *Toy Story* and *Finding Nemo*. He understudied Brandon in 1965's *Race of Hairy Men!* and reconnected with him in Los Angeles. In the 2009 book *Canyon of Dreams: The Magic and Music of Laurel Canyon*, he said, "There was a lot of meeting people and smoking dope and hanging out and hearing music and going to the clubs...All of this came out through Brandon deWilde's desire to be a musician. We'd go to [David] Crosby's place in Laurel Canyon — a funky cabin—and he'd be sitting there with his guitar and singing and Brandon would sometimes jam with him."

In December of 1966, Brandon and Proctor attended

Peter Fonda's marijuana possession trial, with Brandon telling a reporter for the *Citizen News* they were there for moral support. "[Peter] is a good friend and we and Phil are going to form a film production company."

In a 1972 interview quoted in the Sid Griffin book, *Gram Parsons, A Music Biography*, Gram said, "Brandon encouraged us [to come to California]. He got us a job pretending to play in a Peter Fonda movie [*The Trip*] in LA. So we got out of the cold, next door to and near some good country radio stations."

Joey Stec called Brandon, "the most incredible catalyst for musicians in the world." Brandon brought Gram to David Crosby's house, where Gram fell in love with David's girlfriend, Nancy. He also introduced Gram to his business manager, who in turn introduced Gram to Roger McGuinn, which led to Gram joining The Byrds.

Brandon and Gram were the only two of their crowd with money. Both had access to large trust funds, with Gram's coming from a family citrus fruit fortune. Ian Dunlop said that when the new Submarine Band recorded their first album they "went four days without food waiting for it to hit so we could get on tour and make some money. Brandon had a nice big house in Topanga Canyon. We'd go out there and have jam sessions. Brandon would come over and sit at the kitchen table, pick, and sing."

Michael Muentz said, "For Brandon, cocaine and amphetamines were a tool. They were a way of staying up all night and playing music. It could keep you up all night and it wouldn't really interfere with your ability to hold the guitar. He would drink beer, smoke grass to keep the edge off, and this would go on day and night."

Ron Gilbert said, "He liked to stay up late on uppers. We would be up twenty-four hours, and he'd say, 'We're up, we might as well stay up.' It was almost like he was racing not to miss anything. He had a lot of natural energy and I always envied that. He would be playing guitar, writing in his journal.

If he had a choice, I don't think he would ever sleep."

Brandon and Susan's closest neighbor was Ed Freeman, who in a few years would produce the Don McLean album *American Pie*. He was in a band called Joyful Noise and said, "My band members and I often went to Brandon's house to get high." Brandon had a movie projector set up and liked to show footage from road trips and movie sets that he had been capturing since his mid-teens with his Super-8 camera. *In Harm's Way* proved a particularly fertile source of candid clips with appearances by Henry Fonda, Kirk Douglas, and John Wayne.

Ian Dunlop said Brandon was usually working on a script or idea for a short film. He recalled one, "about a guy, driving on a lonely twisting road, thinking about his past and it ends with a dramatic car crash off the road, over a cliff, exploding into a ball of flames."

Dunlop was with Brandon at Peter Fonda's house when Peter and Dennis Hopper talked excitedly about filming America from the back of a motorcycle. As Brandon and Ian left the house, Brandon mentioned he hoped he could become involved in that project.

In the fall of 1967 David Crosby was fired from The Byrds. Tour dates were lined up and the group needed someone to fill in for him. They courted Gram, whose album with the new International Submarine Band, *Safe at Home*, didn't seem to be going anywhere.

Nuese said that the members of the Submarine Band "were trying to figure out what was going to happen, wondering if Gram was only fooling around or acing out of the band. When it looked as though Gram were leaving, Brandon was interested in joining. We had been picking with him for fun, he loved to do it, so why didn't he join the group? We thought that him being a star would help us, and it would be good for him, too. By virtue of the fact that Brandon had a name, it would have gotten us label support.

"He really wanted to do it. His agency at the time was a little stuck up about the whole deal. They didn't think a movie star should be joining a country rock group. So they said no."

In 1963, Brandon was quoted in teen magazines as being happy with how his father had handled his money. But according to Michael Muentz, "There's a strange thing he told me, that he hit the friggin' roof when he finally got his hands on his finances when he turned twenty-one because his father had used a lawyer, not even a financial advisor, a lawyer in Baldwin, to take care of his finances. And instead of investing that money in safe but growth investments – you know this was the period of great growth in our economy, General Motors, AT&T, all these companies were growing, so bonds, some stocks— instead every dime was put into what you classically know as a savings bond. So instead of having that money grow exponentially it was tied up for ten years at less than seven percent. So he was just furious."

Brandon didn't do any better as his trust fund's caretaker. He was too stoned to pay attention to his investments, and, according to Michael Muentz, Brandon, "tried to buy his way into the music business," paying for endless recording sessions involving himself and musician friends.

Brandon's finances were being handled by Larry Spector, accountant/manager to the Los Angeles rock star set of the time and according to Joey Stec, the inspiration for the line in the Flying Burrito Brothers song "Sin City": *On the thirty-first floor your gold-plated door, won't keep out the Lord's burning rain.*

Four years after taking control of a trust fund worth hundreds of thousands of dollars, according to Ralph Scala, Brandon came back from a visit to his accountant "all freaked out. He whipped out a list of what he owed. He lost his house, all his assets...I knew Brandon when he had loads of bucks and when he was penniless."

A spate of television appearances followed. In October of 1968, he taped his second episode (the first was in 1962) of the Western series *The Virginian*, guest-starring with Burgess Meredith, and in December was a banker marooned on a desert island in an episode of the ABC British anthology *Journey to the Unknown*. The next year, he guest-starred on *Hawaii Five-O*, and *Love, American Style*. In February of 1969, he reunited with Julie Harris in the NBC-TV series starring Robert Stack called *The Name of the Game*. In The Bobby Currier Story, Brandon played the title character, a teenage serial killer who is abetted by his girlfriend. Harris played his girlfriend's mother.

In 1968, Joey Stec was 21 and had played guitar for The Association and the psychedelic rock group The Millenium, and had written a single for Denny Doherty of the Mamas and Papas. "I was with Michael Clarke [drummer with The Byrds from 1964 to 1967] at The Troubadour. Chris Hillman was there and he said, 'Hey, do you want to go to Topanga Canyon? This actor friend of ours, Brandon deWilde, is out doing some show but is going to be back late tonight and his buddy Mickey Gauvin is having a party out there.' And I said, 'Sure'.

"It was a great house, secluded as hell. We hung out for ten to twelve hours. When Brandon came in he and I just said, 'Hi' and 'Bye'.

"About four days later, Linda Lawrence, who had a son by Brian Jones, said, 'Hey, I'm going to this cool guy's house. You guys ought to meet.' She said his name was Brandon and I said, 'No way! I was just over there!'"

Joey and Brandon ended up hanging out for about a week. "I didn't have a harmonious environment in my home and Brandon said, 'You know, it's really crazy for you to go driving back every night, stoned, at two o'clock in the morning so why don't you get your stuff and stay.' I came back to my wife's house, took my guitars, my clothes, and I said, 'I'm moving in with Brandon.' Stec said he and Brandon were together "twenty-four/seven for about five months."

"Brandon was born April 9. I'm April 5. We wound up getting our divorces at the same time. We had very similar energies and dressed alike and looked kind of alike. He immediately assumed the role of older brother. He would say, 'Joe, I am five years older than you, so you will listen to me!'" Stec said Brandon also acted like a big brother to Gram. "He would kick Gram's butt. 'Come on, you're not singing from your heart. You're not singing from your stomach. You're like a little sissy.' He used to call him Lou Ella."

Stec said that in the time he spent with Brandon, "I never saw so much creativity served every day on a new platter. The guy was never out of ideas, never out of energy.

"He never surrounded himself with actors. He always surrounded himself just with musicians. Period. He played fairly good guitar and sang fairly well but never disciplined himself to become a musician as he did an actor. Acting he was schooled in, trained, coached, and he dedicated his life to the pursuit of that career. In that music thing it was more like he was a catalyst.

"He introduced me to Leon Russell, Bobby Keys of the Rolling Stones, Keith Richards. He introduced me to the Blues Magoos and I became their guitar player. Chris Hillman, Bonnie & Delaney, Taj Mahal, they would drop by and next thing you know we would sit around and play guitars for three or four hours. Wherever he would go, you would meet someone from him who knew somebody, who knew somebody else, and Brandon would just further the agenda of life."

Stec said that at the Topanga house, Brandon and Susan, "were at each other's throats. They had some kind of arrangement where she stayed downstairs with Jesse and he stayed upstairs and they tried to stay away from each other as much as possible until she was loaded up and ready to get out of there."

On March 22, 1969, under the headline "Parting is Such Sweet Sorrow" the New York *Daily News* ran an old photo of a beaming Brandon and Susan and the caption that Brandon had been sued that day for divorce. Susan, it continued, "now a free-lance writer, asked for custody of their child Jesse, property division and reasonable support."

13

Wild in the sky

"Brandon "got blown out by the divorce," said Joey Stec. "He loved Susan, but that, he was able to handle. The kid, Jesse, broke his heart. He was so blown out by the fact that Jesse was going to have a divorced mother and father. He just loved that kid so much and he had so many fears. He went to pieces."

John Nuese said, "He had down periods when he was real lonely. He wanted to be in love."

Pamela Des Barres, the mega-groupie and singer in Frank Zappa's girl spoof band the GTO's (Girls Together Outrageously), "got a little crush going on Brandon," around this time, according to Joey Stec. "He happened to pass by her street and hold hands with her for a little bit."

Des Barres, author of three delicious memoirs, talked with me in her Santa Monica home about her relationship with Brandon when she was twenty-one and he, six years older.

He was the wildest guy I ever went out with. Triple Aries. He never slept. He was always high on something. He ingested everything known to man.

Maybe the highest time in my life was when I was with him. I did more coke with him than any time in my life. He never seemed to change but I was just gone. On one trip we made to Santa Barbara, we were so coked out I forgot who I was. Literally. I asked Brandon—I remembered his name—'What's my name? Who am I?' He said, 'Go back there and lie down.' So I was lying down in this bus, he had a Volkswagen bus, 'Ohmigod, who am I?' It was just a nightmare.

 He was totally different from anyone I'd ever met. He was walking on a tightrope over flames all the time. He never slept. His eyes were always glittering. Wired... not necessarily high all the time but wired on life.

 He always looked so cool. He wore the best-fitting jeans in the world—always old, tattered, faded, jeans, before it was cool to have them ripped—that he had had for years. He had these suede pants he wore all the time, olive green. They were low slung. So sexy! He had a great shape to his body, which was so funny because I know that as a kid he was chubby. When I knew him, he was very thin. He had a long waist, and when he put weight on maybe it went to his bottom, but when I knew him he didn't have any extra weight at all. He was real wiry and perfect. He was a perfect-looking guy. He was a great-looking guy.

 He was a profound person. When he was in your life, he was in your life. You knew he was there. He was always hard on himself, but I think he was always happy to be alive. He was always hopeful, never depressed. But we were young. He was always a little boy. He was never phony. So honest, almost brutally. Really bright and shining and right there for everybody.

 I just flashed on four different houses I hung out with him in. I helped him find a house right off of Santa Monica Boulevard and La Brea, a really cute little house that he lived in for a while. I went to visit him one time, and I could see he was really out there. He hadn't slept in, like, three days. Nonstop. I don't know how in the hell he did it.

 Right now, the Burritos are legends, but at the time, no one realized how innovative and brilliant it was. He wanted to be part of it. He got it. He understood what they were doing by blending those sounds, and he was real excited about it. He was up all night sometimes, trying to get a certain harmony right. I don't even sing, and he would make me sing with him. We would sit up for hours, trying to get 'I'll Be Your Baby Tonight' in the right harmony.

 I'd be so frustrated. He'd be wide awake and I'd want to go to sleep so bad. And he taped everything.

He was real talented [as a musician]. If he had stayed with it...what happened was he just said, 'oh, fuck it,' and he went back to acting. I think he missed acting. He was doing music too but he gave up the big pursuit of it.

She wrote in her book *I'm with the Band* that they separated because "I couldn't take much more of dear Brandon; he only slept two and a half hours a night, and needed constant adoring care. His blind eyes were wild with a need that no one could fulfill."

Brandon called the modern house he moved into after his divorce, "Concrete and Clay" after the song of the same name. "He just hated it," said Joey Stec. "He loved trees. He always liked to go to the mountains. He would pull up to your house at 11 o'clock at night and say, 'Come on. Get the guitars, let's go to Big Bear.'"

Stec said, "Brandon had a good upbringing. A musician's house wasn't the neatest place in the world but Brandon always kept his houses very clean, the beds were always made. He would have some chickies, Brandon groupies, and they would always take care of his house."

Joey Stec moved in with his new band, the Blues Magoos, as they prepared to go on tour, opening for Herman's Hermits. Second-billed was The Who.

Stec said, "Brandon was a character. He would say, 'Do you want to play some guitars?' And he would load up his Volkswagon camper with amplifiers, guitars, film, cameras, videotape. I swear to God you would think he was going on location. And he would come to your house and he wouldn't leave for four or five days."

Brandon stayed for blocks of time at the house of Peter Tork of The Monkees, where, said Joey Stec, "We had the greatest time of our life. Peter was a great guy and he really loved Brandon." The house had been previously owned by Daryl Dragon, the Captain of the seventies music duo Captain and Tennille, and Wally Cox, character actor and close friend of

Marlon Brando.

Brandon also stayed on the 55-foot boat, and at the home, of his close friend David Crosby. John Nuese called the scene at Crosby's house, "Outrageous — lots of music and drugs. There was a huge swimming pool and I had a standing joke with Brandon over whether it would take ten minutes or two hours before a new girl would take off her bathing suit and jump in."

Ralph Scala: *He was free all the time. We were working and couldn't be that wrecked. For instance, I didn't do coke because I couldn't sing on coke. He didn't have a technical approach to drugs. We were in training, and he was on a leisure cruise. Everyone else did drugs to create. He was into medicine every day. It was his lifestyle.*

John Nuese: *Brandon never shot up. He put lots of stuff up his nose, coke and crystal meth. Every couple of weeks, he would stay up on meth two or three nights at a time.*

Ron Gilbert said, "There was a place called Pink's Hot Dogs and we would drive down in [Brandon's] camper. I used to have a VW bus, where there's nothing in front of you, and Brandon always used to kid me and say how safe his Volkswagon was, a big van with a bubble top, because he had a tire in front. Once I was in the passenger side and he fell asleep. I said, 'Hey!' and grabbed the wheel just in time."

Joey Stec said that the road to Brandon's Topanga Canyon house was "'S' turns and switchbacks all the way and Brandon drove [the van] like a sports car. He used to scare the hell out of me, man. I was never comfortable in that van. It had a vibe that just screamed out, 'Stay away from me!'"

* * *

In early 1970 Brandon filmed his first movie in five years, *The Deserter*, playing a young officer who joins a suicide mission against the Apaches and dies in the arms of his captain. He had sixth billing, after Chuck Connors, Ricardo Montalban, Richard Crenna, Ian Bannen and Bekim Fehmiu.

Director Burt Kennedy told me, "I knew him from *Goodbye, My Lady*, where I had visited the set because I was friends with the producers. I met him now and then over the years. I'd run into him in restaurants. He was always in trouble with the girls. He was handsome and didn't know it.

"I didn't think he'd do the role; it was such a small part. But he said 'Sure.' The picture was supposed to be a Steve McQueen vehicle. To get me to direct, they told me McQueen would do it.

"As a kid Brandon was very strange. In *Shane*—the way his head would bob back and forth. He was a funny little kid. He was an awful good actor for a kid actor. Most of them turn out to be real brats. He was maturing and had all the qualifications. He was great in *Hud*. In *The Deserter* he was very youthful looking. He looked like he was in his early twenties. And a really good actor. In some scenes, every once in a while, he showed that he was just as sensitive as he had been."

Pat Wayne was in the cast. Five years earlier, his father John Wayne had starred with Brandon in *In Harm's Way*. Pat described the filming of his own movie with Brandon in a letter to the author: *We were on location for approximately 12 weeks. In Spain we filmed in two different places of the Costa Del Sol. In Torremolinos we were constantly plagued with dense fog. And unfortunately the topography was critical to the story so we had to wait patiently until we could film. The filming in Italy occurred at the old Dino DeLaurentis studio. Living in Rome with per diem is as close to Heaven on earth as there is.*

The film was, potentially, a very commercial western with good production and direction values. It wasn't a box office success. I think one of the main reasons for the failure was this: The cast, an ensemble of highly visible Hollywood luminaries, was headed by a talented, attractive Yugoslavian actor named Bekim Fehmiu. He was an unknown but had some heat from having just starred in two other unreleased features. The powers that be assumed that he was headed for stardom. It didn't happen and neither did the film.

When I first saw Brandon on the set I remember thinking to myself how much he had changed since I had last seen him. Physically he had the typical look of a hippie—long stringy dirty hair, dirty worn clothing, maybe even love beads although I couldn't swear to it.

On the set he was very pleasant, very personable, and very professional in his work. On a film, especially on location, cast members tend to be one happy family, interacting socially apart from work. But off the set Brandon tended to be a loner, spending his time alone or with his girlfriend who visited for a brief period during the filming.

Generally speaking everyone liked him and would have welcomed his company. My guess is he felt disconnected for some reason from us. One final note: In the '60s when you saw someone dressed the way Brandon did you assumed they were involved in the use of illegal controlled stimulants— druggies. I never saw him behave in a way that would suggest that he was under the influence either on or off the set.

Brandon sounded at peace in a magazine interview he gave while filming the movie: "For years I've had the feeling that there was a man inside that small boy struggling to get out. I can't tell you how glad I felt when I walked onto this set wearing my uniform for the first time and all the actors stood up and gave me a big cheer, with the loudest, phoniest applause you could imagine. At least none of them said, 'well, here comes the kid.'

"I'm hoping I can combine music and acting as a career. Like a lot of people I used to spend my time worrying about what used to be and things that probably won't ever happen. My new philosophy is NOW. It's the only thing that truly affects a person's future."

Ian Dunlop had ditched the LA music scene for a life of farming and fishing in Cornwall, England. Brandon dated a Danish girl while filming *The Deserter,* and when the movie wrapped, the couple visited her friends in Holland, then swung by Cornwall during the 1970 Christmas season.

Dunlop and Brandon hadn't seen each other for two years. They recorded a few songs in a studio in Dunlop's home. "He told me *The Deserter* was so corny," Dunlop told the author. "He felt it took absolutely no acting ability. I remember him doing his final scene, facetiously putting ketchup all over one Indian, and an arrow through his hat, crawling up to the cavalry officer, saying, 'Did I do good?' 'Bang!' and 'They give me money for doing that.'"

Brandon spent a few months kicking around England. Back in America, John Nuese said, "A real good drummer would come over and play. His wife was pissed he was there all the time. She called the police and said, 'The folks at the house are dealing drugs to neighborhood kids.' People had been over until 3:00 a.m. and Brandon had been up for several days. He took his phone off the hook and went to sleep.

"Plainclothes cops in construction hats stormed in, found a half ounce of grass and two-tenths of a gram of coke. They busted into my bedroom, saying, 'If you move we'll blow your f---- head off.' They made quite a to-do over it when they found out who Brandon was.

"In the cop car, we were singing Charlie Pride's 'I'm Busted.' We were fingerprinted and put in the Van Nuys jail. Peter Fonda bailed us out four hours later. When we got back, Brandon said, 'They didn't find all our stash. Let's get high!'"

Michael Muentz said, "He called me and said he needed a lawyer and I get him this superstar lawyer Harry Weiss. I had actually been to a party in his house and it was like being at the Museum of Modern Art. He looked like Salvador Dali and he was the most famous drug lawyer in Lost Angeles. Brandon told me that he didn't want any cash payment. What he wanted was one of the miniature boats from *In Harm's Way*."

The court appearance for the drug bust was the last time John Nuese saw Brandon.

* * *

Brandon had moved out of the "concrete and clay" house. "He didn't have a place to live," said Michael Muentz. "I asked my landlord if he had anything and he said, 'Yes, he had a little ranch-style, two-bedroom house in Tarzana in the San Fernando Valley.' The rent was $250 a month.

"Brandon didn't have anybody living with him at the time so he says to me and my wife, 'Why don't you two come live with me?' Because he didn't like to be alone. That was his biggest thing.

"Next thing you know he pops up with Linda Lawrence, who came with her son Julian Jones, who was like six years old. This was Dennis the Menace and not fun to be around. We look out the window one morning and we see him playing with some stick and a moving object, look closer, and he's playing with a stick and rattlesnake in the car park.

Muentz said, as an example of how cutting Brandon could be to his friends and particularly to girlfriends, "He takes Linda to Joshua Tree, where Gram and he used to go and take peyote, and he was going to stay there for a week and he comes back after a day and a half, stumbles out of the car laughing his head off, but it wasn't funny, and says, 'She doesn't talk! Imagine going to the desert with somebody who doesn't talk!' So she didn't stay long."

Kay Poorboy was a dancer at the Hollywood strip club, the Classic Cat. She came to Los Angeles from Tulsa with Leon Russell one night and was living with him. She had also dated Eric Burden and Joe Cocker.

Muentz recalled that Kay was at Brandon's house "with this cute-looking girl, and I just see how she's looking at him. After a few minutes I catch him alone and I say, 'Brandon, be careful.' And he grabs her by the hand, pulls me in front of her and says, 'Michael says I should be careful of you.'

"Within a few hours he told me, 'It's time for you and your wife to move out because Janice is going to come live with me.'"

14

Janice

"I called him Brand," said Janice Gero, the woman who would become his second wife, in one of a series of telephone interviews with me in early 2012. "I didn't even know he was an actor. I thought he was a musician, because musicians were always coming in and out of the house. And I thought he was pretty high up there because he was friends with people like The Beatles." Brandon showed her a film clip of him chasing George, Ringo, Paul, and John on a beach in the Bahamas with a spear and then being chased by them, in turn. "Occasionally he would say, 'I have a job I have to do. I'll be back soon.' I always thought it was doing music."

Janice's first inkling that the star of movies, theater, and television for twenty of his twenty-seven years had even acted came a few months into their living together. Brandon and Susan's son, Jesse, spent months at a time with each parent because Susan lived a long plane ride away, in Alaska with her second husband. One evening, Janice, Brandon, and Jesse "were all casually piled up on the couch watching TV, and *Night Gallery* came on. Rod Serling was the host and he used to give a little promo about the episode, and he mentioned Brandon deWilde.

I turned around and looked up at Brandon and said, 'What are *you* doing on the television?' All he said was, 'Oh good, maybe I'll get some royalties off of that.'"

Janice grew up in a "very old-fashioned and grounded" family in San Fernando Valley where her father worked for Lockheed as an electrical engineer and her mother was a homemaker. In a note to the author, she described her upbringing like this: "We lived a very lean life. I remember things like my mother making me clothes from sheets. We also had a car with a hole in the floorboard so we could see the road passing under our feet. However, we lived a rich life. We danced in the livingroom to music from Big Country and Fantasia and at Christmas made popcorn balls and hung socks for stockings. We had a squeaky clean house always in order and neat as a pin. So while we were actually poor I never felt it until I was a teenager. Then I noticed my friends went to the prom, had class rings, and many had cars. I had none of those things."

Janice graduated from high school at sixteen, having skipped a couple of grades, and appeared in TV commercials with Mickey Rooney and print ads for the You Got Milk campaign. She was studying fashion design at the Los Angeles School of the Arts. Everything changed when her father was killed and her mother grievously injured in a car crash. "My personal life was in so much trauma. I was just trying to take care of myself as a teenage girl. I was finding a way to get by."

The Classic Cat was a strip club frequented by the likes of Steve McQueen, Jim Morrison, and Lana Turner and featured in a camera pan of the Sunset Strip that opens *The Trip*. "A friend who danced there said, 'You can make spectacular money,' which, oh my gosh, you could. You could make five, six, seven hundred dollars a night. Especially if you headlined. And I did headline. I was one of the featured dancers because I sang."

"I was real tiny, weighed probably 102 pounds, very flat-chested. Ninety-five percent of my act was taking off my gloves.

I would take forever to take off these gloves that went from my fingertips all the way to my armpit. That was my gimmick. Stupid, but back in those days, strippers were truly strippers. There was an art to it."

A few months into the job, "I had spent the night at another dancer's house in North Hollywood who ran with a crowd of musicians like the Flying Burrito Brothers. I had taken a shower and wrapped myself in a towel and was standing in front of the mirror, brushing my hair, when the door flew open. I whirled around, stunned, and my towel fell off. So," she said with a characteristic easy laugh, "When I met Brandon, I met him with no clothes on whatsoever."

Brandon "turned about eighteen shades of pale. When I walked out into the living room, he was like, 'I'm so sorry.' I said, 'That's OK,' and he said, 'Hey, I'm Brandon,' and I said, "I'm Janice.'" They quickly discovered a mutual love for music, and Janice said that except for a couple of weeks early in the relationship, "I don't remember from that day ever really leaving him."

"He was a really creative, sweet, deep, sometimes troubled young man, and he adored his son. The divorce was extraordinarily hard on him. According to the way he talked about it, the parents sided with the girl. They felt he should have stayed with her. When he lost her, he lost a lot. Even though he was at a low point in his life, I loved him like crazy, and I think he appreciated that."

Janice moved into his ranch house in the San Fernando Valley.

"He smoked pot a bit, and he didn't do coke because who could afford it? He liked peyote or mescaline. But he was big on speeders. He was a bit of a pill popper. My drug of choice was downers. So I was always sleeping and he was always awake. I had my demons I was running from, so I would take downers and sleep, and he had his demons he was running from, so he would take speeders and literally stay up for forty-eight hours, writing, writing, writing. He had to get his thoughts out. And with me sleeping and him speeding we didn't have much of a life.

"After about thirty days of living like that, I couldn't do it anymore, and I went home to my mother's house to clean up. And his promise to me was that he would do the same thing. By the time I got back after a couple of weeks, he had stopped. That was a turning point with us. There weren't as many people going in and out of the house. It was as though our life slowed down a whole bunch. He didn't do any drugs that I knew of after that for the two years that I knew him.

"We met each other and had the courage between the two of us to say 'Listen, we're both going to give up on our crutches and trust and depend on each other.'"

Ralph Scala said that Brandon "couldn't unlock the door so the door was always open. He couldn't count change. He could barely drive. From the house to his getting the car started could easily take forty-five minutes. He was blind without his contact lenses, and helping him put them in was a major occupation." Janice "helped him as much as she could. She was a mother and manager to him."

Michael Muentz said that Janice, "was the first girl to grab him by the neck and have him where she wanted him and he loved that: 'Finally, somebody knows how to handle me.'"

Janice said, "I'm very much a Capricorn, and he's very much an Aries. He made me more adventurous than I was, and I think I made him more grounded than he was."

She said that when Brandon first came to the strip club to see her, "He said, 'I don't want you up there. You're done.' He was like, 'You could be doing something else, not that.' I loved to sing and we decided to write songs together."

Janice and Brandon did just that, Janice singing their rockabilly-influenced tunes to the accompaniment of a band that featured Brandon on his acoustic twelve-string Martin guitar. "He played beautifully. The man could really play the guitar," she said. The hole-in-the-wall clubs in and outside of Los Angeles paid a fraction of what Janice made dancing or Brandon made acting. "We were so poor we went to the grocery store and were actually taking bags of beans and were putting them inside our clothes to get something to eat. I never forgot it because I had never stolen anything."

Since her parents' car crash, Janice was skittish about being in cars and she said that Brandon "would put on his black glasses and drive like a grandpa." Nonetheless, on the Hollywood Freeway one day, "I leaned over to get something on the floor, and then he leaned over, and he smashed into the car in front of us. I ended up dislocating both of my knees. I asked him why he did that, and he said, 'Oh, the front of your dress was falling.' He bent over so he could see down the front of my dress! I said, 'Brandon! Are you crazy? You're with me all the time!'"

"Truly, we were so madly in love with each other."

She said, "When I found out he was an actor, I was very optimistic and encouraged him to get back into it again and he was like, 'I'm not sure I want to.' Not that he didn't enjoy being a child star, but rather than him being hugely confident because of the experiences he had, they made him question who he was. He was not comfortable with that part of his life because he didn't feel he was known for who he really was."

His parents, whom she never met, "didn't appreciate his lifestyle. They felt he needed to be in New York. I appreciate that because he was a gifted actor, but he needed to do that on his own. As a child, they had framed his life and for a very long time, they dictated his future. He told himself, 'I'm going to step out of the light a little bit until I can get my head turned out right.' I give him a lot of credit for doing that, because not many do."

By the middle of 1971, "The acting jobs were offered to him, and he finally felt, 'OK, I could do this.'" On August 16, he signed a three-year contract with the William Morris Agency, listing his parents' apartment on Eighty-Sixth Street as his address. Soon after that, Brandon took the starring role in a San Diego repertory theater production of *Butterflies Are Free*, which had been a hit on Broadway three years earlier. Brandon's character was a blind man who becomes independent with the help of a loving girl and in spite of a good-intentioned but smothering mother. Marjorie Lord from TV's *Make Room for Daddy* played the mother.

"We were so happy he was doing something, and we all went to see him," said Ralph Scala.

Ron Gilbert said, "In *Hud* there's a scene in the café with his grandfather where he's piling all this stuff on his hamburger, and the grandfather says 'You're going to eat all that stuff?' and he says, 'I am.' That's the way Brandon really ate. I think he brought honesty to his roles." He said Brandon "was electrifying" in his new role. "There was one scene where Brandon is having a fight with his girlfriend and loses his orientation. He opens a door, and it's supposed to smack him in his head. You do the old trick of putting your foot in front of the door and making a smack sound, but the way he did it was so realistic, the audience gasped."

Pamela Des Barres came to a performance, accompanied by her new boyfriend, Don Johnson, about twelve years before he came to personify 1980s hipness in *Miami Vice*. "Brandon was straight. I thought, 'Well, that's really cool. I'm really proud of him.' He was totally sober. But he wasn't different. That was the amazing thing. He was still so full of life."

Janice said, "His hope was that he would make money with music, but becoming a musician was like breaking into a whole new field. He ended up going into theater because that's what he'd been doing all along and he had more opportunity there, had a broader foundation of people he knew. He was coming back into acting clean, and he was really happy about it. He had a very neat style all of his own and I think he thought, 'I am going to do music and I'm going to be an actor.'" The San Diego production of *Butterflies Are Free* "was his segue into confidence. It was small but it was received really, really well. It was his way to put his foot back in the water and say 'I'm OK with this— I *can* swim.''

Ralph Scala said, "Sometimes you take a turn and get lost. He was lost for a while. He was on his way back."

* * *

Brandon's parents, said Janice, "were very, very much against him marrying me." Ron Gilbert recalled seeing a letter they wrote their son. Brandon "had been up for a few days and he dragged this thing out. It was pretty dog-eared. It hurt ME and they weren't even my parents. I don't know if I could say those things to my kids. They told him he had screwed up his career and his life. They said that every time he had to make a decision on his own, it had been a bad one.

"They alluded to the drug bust and his legal problems. The letter said, 'If you marry this woman we will have nothing more to do with you.'" According to Gilbert, "I think [marrying Janice] was a life raft out there and if he didn't grab onto it, he would sink."

* * *

Steady work as an actor funded a move to a luxurious one-bedroom apartment in a Spanish-style complex in North Hollywood and Brandon and Janice were married in front of the large living-room fireplace on March 25, 1972. "I never was a diamond girl, but I love opals," Janice said, "and Brandon went and had a ring made for me with gold leaves and flower petals, and in the center of the flower is an opal, aquamarine like the ocean in the Caribbean." Brandon also found a seamstress to turn a fashion sketch of Janice's into a wedding dress, lacy white with a full skirt, long sleeves, and a high neck and festooned with tiny aquamarine flowers. Janice's mother, who had sewn the couple's living-room drapes from a pair of sheets, was in charge of the food for the wedding reception and, in typical frugal fashion, provided a small cake, nuts and mints, and alcohol-free punch.

There were about twenty-five guests, including Gram Parsons, who best man Ron Gilbert said shocked everyone when he turned up weighing, "like three-hundred pounds."

For their honeymoon, Janice and Brandon spent a week and a half driving along the Southern California coastline in Brandon's 1969 blue Ford Econoline. The van had a pop-up roof for comfortable walking-around room, a kitchenette, and a double bed that pulled out of the couch. "You could be parked on the beach with the doors open, lying down on the bed and facing the sun coming up in front of you. You can't get a hotel that's better than that," Janice said.

That month, Brandon's face dominated the publicity posters for the movie *Wild in the Sky* under the banner headline "Come along for the ride Baby—You're gonna love it!" Brandon played an anti-war activist who escapes with two other prisoners by hijacking a B-52 bomber. He was described in a trade publicity booklet as "A former child star who breathes much easier now that he has amassed a strong backlog of adult roles."

Scala said, "Brandon's marriage seemed to be working. He got heavily into the metaphysical comprehension of existence—Buddha, Zen, I Ching, Tarot cards. He got somewhat organized, got money from cutting corners and paid some bills and took up *Butterflies Are Free* and got rave reviews."

Brandon signed on to a larger and more prestigious production of the play that starred Maureen O'Sullivan as the mother and, as the girlfriend, Karen Grassle, who would portray Michael Landon's wife on *Little House on the Prairie* a few years later. The play was scheduled for a two-week run in Denver's Elitch Theater where the manager was Chris Kirkland, who, if he had remained John Henry way back when, might have forestalled Brandon's acting career.

Director John Going said in an interview with the author on

May 9, 1989, "Brandon had done [*Butterflies Are Free*] for another repertory group earlier, but the experience seemed all very new to him. He seemed very excited about starting a new chapter in his life. I find that when an actor has done the play before, it is a little tricky. They are used to doing things a certain way. But Brandon was very, very amenable to trying new things he hadn't done before and joining in on the concept I had. He was very hardworking. I had a lot of admiration for him for that.

"I knew of Brandon as a child actor, and I was very curious to see what he was like. Sometimes your child stars are a special breed of human being. But Brandon was a very, very sweet man. As a child actor I thought his instincts were very fine, very genuine, very true. He had been so natural. Often that's the problem with kids who act. Children should be the best actors in the world because they're so good at playing games and imagining. They have no inhibitions, nothing they're trying to cover up. But people get hold of them, acting coaches, and they don't understand what it is about the process of acting that is so fetching. But all the qualities Brandon had as a child actor were still there.

"There was also something a little sad about him. You felt he had been through a lot of stuff. I sensed that his life had not been a bed of roses. He was either in the process of conquering something or had just conquered something."

15

Butterflies are free

During the two-week run of the play, The *Denver Post* ran a photo of a beaming Brandon and Janice outside the Elitch Theater. Janice said that when she first met Brandon, "His cheeks were all hollow. He was just drained, God bless his heart. If you see those pictures of us in the parking lot, he just looked beautiful, so happy, a twinkle in his eye and a big ol' smile on his face. He was getting healthy, putting some weight back."

The play's last performance was on July 1. A few days later, "We put Jesse on the airplane to go home to Alaska, and [Brandon] had arranged for us to go horseback-riding. I didn't horseback ride but Brandon did. He loved horses. He was a little bit of a cowboy at heart." The couple planned to drive back to Los Angeles the next day, July 6. "In the middle of the night, I woke up shrieking. I actually had a tumor-sized cyst on my ovaries, which ruptured, and I was bleeding internally." Brandon drove Janice to the Colorado General Hospital. "He signed the papers to have the surgery done, and I just remember him saying, 'You're going to be fine. I have a good doctor.'

"I'd come out of surgery, and the phone rang. He had gone back to the hotel to pack us up, and he said, 'I'm on my way. I'm bringing you a present.'"

According to the *Denver Post*, at 3:25 p.m. in the suburb of Lakewood, Brandon's van struck a guardrail, then caromed into a flatbed construction truck that was parked on the side of the road. The driver of the truck, twenty-one-year-old Alan James Hein, wasn't injured. The Jaws of Life extricated Brandon from the wreck, and he was raced to St. Anthony's Hospital. He had a broken neck, back, and leg.

Janice said, "They told me my husband had been in a severe accident, he had a puncture in his aorta, but that he was still alive, and they were going to transport me in an ambulance to the hospital where he was in because he had asked for me. When I got there, he had already died." The official time of death was 7:20 p.m.

She said, "Between my pain from surgery, and heartache, they kept me fairly medicated. I remember being in a stupor most of the time." But she clearly remembered this: "I said, 'I can't leave [Denver]. Brandon had a present for me in the car.'" At the junkyard, in the wreckage of the flattened van, she somehow found the presents Brandon had alluded to in their last conversation: a bouquet of flowers and an eight-track recording of their favorite song, "Lean on Me." "I turned twenty-one in January, I was married in March and he was killed in July. He was there, and then he was gone."

Janice said that when Brandon crashed his van it was raining hard and it was likely he hadn't slept since checking her into the hospital at around midnight. "Somebody said he was drugged, that he was drinking, and I said, that is the biggest lie ever. The poor guy had put his son on an airplane and his wife was bleeding internally and rushed into surgery, and Brandon was freaked out, trying to get to his wife." His death "was a double loss" because she never saw Jesse again.

Michael Muentz said he has come to appreciate Janice's good influence on his buddy. "I don't know if [their marriage] would have lasted any further than the eight year length of his first marriage but for those two years that he was with her he was sober and getting back to his career as his number one priority."

Joey Stec was looking after Brandon's house while Brandon was out of town, and was recording at the legendary studio in Van Nuys, Sound City, when the phone rang in the control room. "I said to the receptionist, 'Do you mind? I told you we don't want any calls in here,' and she said, 'You're going to want to take this one.'" Stec said that when he took the call from the hospital in Denver, he was wearing Brandon's cowboy shirt.

On July 6, Ron Gilbert was in the studio mixing material for an album Brandon and he had worked on together. "My wife called me and said, 'Brandon's been killed.' I said, 'What? Are you kidding me?' She said, 'Come home. We're all over at Ralph's house.' Everyone was just sitting around in a state of shock. It was like a wake. We would drink, talk, hash it over. We had no information. It was like, 'He was killed on a highway, yeah.' You can never prepare for something like that."

Fritz's old friend Bruce Laffey said, "I had been living in the Caribbean, working in a restaurant, and I was serving some people. Some guy sitting at the counter said, 'Gee, isn't it too bad about that kid actor who died today?' I knew it couldn't be Brandon, but I thought 'Oh, Jesus' and I said, 'Who?' And he said, 'I can't think of his name. Oh, God, what's his name? You know, the one who was in *Shane.*'

"It was something awful the way Fritz and Genie heard about his accident. Some doctor called, and it was just so cold. Somebody said something about, there's a guy in the hospital here, his name is deWilde…It was just slapped at them. Nobody took the time to prepare them." Laffey said that Brandon's parents didn't make it to the hospital in time.

On July 7, 1972, the William Morris Agency sent a letter to the union for television and radio artists, cc'd to the west coast branch of William Morris, Actor's Equity and the Screen Actor's Guild. "Dear Connie," it states, "Please be advised that our client Brandon DeWilde is deceased as of July 6, 1972.

Please mark your records accordingly."

* * *

"There was a row," said Ron Gilbert. "The parents didn't want anyone coming to the funeral. I told Janice, 'Oh no, this can't be. I appreciate their feelings, but I've got to be there.' Janice said, 'Don't worry. I'm in charge.'

"Gram was staying at the Chateau Marmont. I called him up to tell him Brandon had died. Ralph told me Gram didn't want to be bugged by it. He told Ralph, 'Ronnie is pressuring me to come to his funeral.' Musing on Gram not wanting to attend the funeral of such a close friend, Gilbert said, "I guess he was into drugs. It's the only thing I can think of."

Janice said the money from Brandon's insurance policy all went to five-year-old Jesse. "I had nothing and I was left with the expenses...there were huge medical bills." Coming into Elitch's next was Mickey Rooney in an English comedy *See How They Run*. "He knew me and he knew Brandon," Janice said of the actor and it was announced in *Variety* that proceeds from Mickey Rooney's July 14th matinee performance would be split between Janice and an education fund for Jesse.

The memorial service was held July 13. Janice arranged for it to be at the Nichiren Shoshu Temple because Brandon had practiced Buddhism. She acknowledged that his Catholic parents "were not very happy about that."

Ron Gilbert was not happy about it either. "The service was just a joke. It was in a Buddhist temple all the way out in Orange County. None of the Hollywood community came. I felt very bad—terrible. It could have been...Brandon was a star. He was in a classic movie. *Shane* was a classic movie. Some of the people who wrote tributes to him in the newspaper, Julie Harris, for instance, would have come. I'm sure Paul Newman would have come if it had been a little more convenient."

Janice does not recall seeing Brandon's parents at the funeral.

Ralph Scala does, describing them as, "people of style. They reminded me of what we used to call old money." He said, "The father had a real worn face. I could tell they were really pissed off at us. They were very upset with his failure in his career and didn't want to associate with the people they associated with that failure. He died with his low-life friends, according to them. He didn't know our value. We were just the people who had killed him. They were upset because the last words they said to their son were harsh words. I remember wishing there was something I could say to comfort them. I wanted to tell his parents how much I loved Brandon, and I went over to them and just started to cry. They were a little cold and standoffish at first. When they saw everyone crying their eyes out they were moved."

Joey Stec said he and Brandon, "used to go to this place called Nudie's, that had the most expensive, coolest cowboy shirts in all L.A. Brandon had just bought this cream-colored gabardine with black silk trimming on it and smiley button pockets. There was a line of people walking by his casket and when I got there, I reached down, put a guitar pick in his left pocket, clipped the pocket closed, and said, 'There, buddy,' because he always wanted to be a musician."

Brandon was cremated. Janice said, "I bought a double niche for he and I in a cemetery in Sun Valley where my father was buried, and his urn was placed there."

* * *

A few months after Brandon's death Janice received boxes of memorabilia from Brandon's aunt. "Old photo albums and every newspaper clipping. That's when I found out all the things he had done. 'Oh my gosh, he knew this person and that person.'" At twenty-two, she was up for the role of Honey in a touring production of *Lenny*. A mention by gossip columnist Rona Barrett in the *Los Angeles Times* that Janice would be carrying on the deWilde acting legacy "freaked me out" and prompted her to withdraw from the role, and acting. At twenty-five, she married the road manager for Kiss, and Earth, Wind and Fire. Their daughter contracted spinal meningitis and encephalitis at three months old. Desperate to save her, Janice began studying early neurological development. When her daughter recovered, she filed for divorce and left Hollywood for Georgia. "I thought, 'there are too many temptations and too many bad roads I could head down, so I need to get out of here. This is not a good place for me to raise a child.'" In Georgia, she built on her studies of early brain development to start a Christian school to help "socially quirky" children, such as those with Asperger's, autism, and dyslexia.

Janice is still in Georgia, running a similar Christian academy that she also started. She has been happily married for twenty years and has three children and five grandchildren. She calls Brandon "the love of my life."

Director Burt Kennedy called Brandon's death "bad timing. If he had not been killed he would have finally found the part to put him over. He was good-looking yet could do the rough stuff, like an older River Phoenix. Perfect leading man—he looked young, and everything turned to youth about the time he died."

Michael Muentz said that Brandon, "made this horrible trade-off, neglecting his career for just having someone to play guitar with. They were all flattered. But the cost to him was that he was completely detached from all his movie buddies, Dean Stockwell, Peter Fonda, by the time he died. He was doing *Butterflies are Free* because he was trying to crawl his way back up the ladder. He died because he was forced to do summer stock."

On the morning of September 19, 1973, Gram Parsons was found dead in a room at the Joshua Tree Inn. He was twenty-six and the cause of death was listed as heart failure. A posthumous album of Gram's released in 1974 was his second solo effort, called *Grievous Angel* and compiled from 1973 recordings. "In My Hour of Darkness," was written by Gram and Emmylou Harris and contains a lyric about a strong young man driving through the night and a deadly Denver bend.

Alan Ladd died of a drug overdose in 1964 at the age of fifty, only ten years after he tenderly exhorted Brandon to "grow up strong and straight" and to "look after your parents —both of them."

John Roberts wrote in *Hollywood Studio*, "The lives and careers for both Ladd and deWilde ended sadly. Ladd at least accomplished superstardom while deWilde suffered the classic dilemma of a child star trying to succeed as an adult actor. De Wilde demonstrated in a handful of performances that he was an outstanding child actor but juvenile triumphs count for little in the adult world."

In Brandon's obituaries, it is as though the 1960s never happened—that his teenage years were not upended, like the country itself, by the assassinations of the Kennedys and Martin Luther King, the war in Vietnam and the youth riots in Chicago and Watts, rock music and drugs—but that he was always an innocent child in a simpler time. The *New York Times*' obituary read: "As a poised, precocious tow-headed 7-year-old making his debut on Broadway in 1950 Brandon deWilde received the kind of reviews from critics and raves from audiences that experienced actors yearn for.

"Often because he continued to look younger than his age he played the role of the ingenious youth learning the bitterness of life. The professionals he worked with praised him for an unpretentiousness that many found a surprising quality in one so celebrated from his earliest years.

"In his later years he took courses at the New School and once said that he was interested in other pursuits besides acting."

Lester Polakov said, "After *Emperor's Clothes* I lost track of Brandon. The theater is like that. There were fifty people in *Member of the Wedding*. You see them every day. Have your meals with them, go on the road, and sleep with them, see them day and night. Then the show closes, and two weeks later, you see them on Broadway and say, 'Now, wasn't that…?' When he died, I just thought, "Someone so talented and promising, where he might have gone to and what he would have done had he lived." Robert Whitehead said, "There was nothing neurotic about him. He never seemed discouraged or in pain. He was just a darling little boy. I thought he would outlive us all."

In an essay printed in the August 4, 1972, *New York Times*, Julie Harris wrote: *I just felt when I knew he was gone that I had to tell him this again. I don't know why we feel compelled to reach out this way. What does it mean if people read what I feel about Brandon—I don't know! But now we have to remember him. And he was such a gifted actor. And we who loved him were so proud of the things he did.*

…All those long months we were a family and he was the heart of us. The most loving, adorable golden boy. Our joyful adventures went on and on. Miss Waters, Brandon and I became one person—all of us in the play really. I can hear the quality of wonder in his voice, even now, when he said to Ethel, holding to her ear a big seashell, 'You want to listen to the ocean?' He was a real artist: He knew where the laughs were and he knew where the sadness was, too. And his devoted mother and father gave him the help he needed to play all those months.

As Teresa says to her Leslie at the end of Brendan Behan's The Hostage *I say to Brandon, 'I'll never forget you Brandon. Never! Till the end of time.'*

John Anderson said the deWildes "were crushed over Brandon's death. Crushed that it happened to their very beloved boy. They talked about Brandon a lot, about his life and their memories of him. The talk always came back to *The Member of the Wedding*. They had warm memories of that time." Fritz, Robert Whitehead said, "had always been serious, but fun. He was lively. He liked life, liked drinking and girls. After Brandon's death, he became strangely serious. It just took something out of both of them that never found its way back again." Genie, according to Lou Peterson, "sort of disappeared. She wouldn't call people and didn't want to talk about it and when she did talk about it she was exceedingly bitter." Martha Carson said, "I told her that a friend of mine lost her husband and got some comfort in writing thank-you cards to the sympathy notes. There were so many for Brandon, people sending in prayers from all over the world, but she said she didn't get any comfort from that at all."

Bruce Laffey said, "Fritz had a show at the Music Box theater. He called me and said 'We'll have dinner because you haven't met Jesse yet, and Genie said, 'Be prepared. You're going to be shocked when he comes in.' And a little Brandon deWilde ran in the door. Little glasses, blond hair, the whole thing. I couldn't believe it. It was frightening. He said, 'Tell me some more things about my father.'"

Janice said that a few years after Brandon's death, someone contacted her on his parents' behalf, saying that they wanted him to be buried in their family plot, and could they please have his ashes. She said no. "Then life started going on for me and they requested again and my mom said to me, 'Listen, he is all they had, he was their only son,' and I said, 'Fine.'"

Fritz died in 1980. He was sixty-six-years-old. Genie had a second hip operation in the early 1980s that left her on crutches and she died of cancer on Memorial Day in 1987. The three now rest in the same plot of land, about twenty minutes from Baldwin at Pinelawn Memorial Park in Farmingdale, New York. Genie and Brandon share a headstone.

Lyle Bettger closed a letter to the author like this: "Perhaps if I sat and dwelled on the memories for a couple of weeks I might do better but I can't do that. It is a kind of sad end, after such a promising start. A lovely small family that just seemed to fall apart from things over which they had no control."

Acknowledgements

I am indebted to each of the following correspondents. I hope that with *All Fall Down*, I have done justice to their kindness to me, and to their memory of Brandon.

Author Interviews, 2011-2012

Janice deWilde, Maarten Heybroek, Richard Burns, Dr. Maurice (Jay) Smith, Michael Muentz, George Stevens, Jr., Joey Stec

Author Interviews, 1988-1991

Relatives: Audrey deWilde Ford
Baldwin associates: Kenneth Schmidt, Greg Murphy, Rick Williams, Florence Reis, Helene Light, Glenn Sitterly
Member of the Wedding associates: Julie Harris, Robert Whitehead, Lou Peterson, Terry Fay, Lester Polakov, Oliver Rea
Music friends and associates: Josh White Jr., Dick Rosmini, Pamela Des Barres, Jon Corneal, Ron Gilbert, Jon Nuese, Ian Dunlop, Peppy Castro, Ralph Scala
Acting friends and associates: Tommy Rettig, Ed Robbins, Haila Stoddard, Chris Kirkland, Paul Newman, Gary Merrill, John Going, Burt Kennedy
Friends of Eugenia and Frederic deWilde: Margaret Garland, John Anderson, Martha Carson, Lyle Bettger, John Gillespie, Janet Hill, Henry Moritz, Bruce Laffey

Written Correspondence
Relatives: June Berry, Ann Wolfe Evans
Baldwin associates: George Voigt
Acting associates: Patricia Neal, Pat Wayne, Chuck Connors, Helen Hayes, Fred Zinnemann

Music associates: Roger McGuinn, Norman Gimbel, Ed Freeman

Friends of Eugenia and Frederic deWilde: Mary Neal Huffaker, William Dyer, Carolyn Tierney, Mrs. John Marshal Glass, J. Brandon Price, Lyle Bettger, John Anderson

Serendipity came my way for this second edition, as it had for the first when I was contacted by a Roman priest with the contact information for Janice. This time, the angel was Michael Muentz. After reading my book, where he was mentioned only as the "Mike" who taught Brandon guitar, Muentz identified himself as Brandon's best friend in his late teen years, and he patiently fleshed out for me Brandon's shift from actor to musician. He also put me in touch with Joey Stec, the best friend who bookended Brandon's adult life. Brandon was lucky to have two such devoted, loving people in his life and it is my luck that they both have phenomenal memories.

This second edition is also enriched by Greg Murphy, for lending me letters that Brandon wrote him when they were childhood buddies, and by Robert "Bo" Smith, who made me the beneficiary of his astonishing knowledge of film with the gift of a long (slightly embarrassing to me) list of corrections.

Thank you, as always, to my husband, Don McLean. Thank you to Wyatt McLean and Jackie McLean for their encouragement in the long process of refining my manuscript, as well as help editing copy and selecting photos. I am grateful to Jane and David from Custom Museum Publishing, and to don Gianni, Richard Burns, and Maarten Heybroek for allowing me to reproduce their personal photographs.

A special thank you to Tony Reznak, Jr. for his generosity, wise insights, publicity, photographs, superb proof-reading, and also for keeping the memory of Brandon alive so splendidly with the website RememberingBrandon.net.

Bibliography

The Member of the Wedding. Carson McCullers. Houghton Mifflin Company, 1946.

The Best Plays of 1949-1950. Edited by John Chapman. Dodd, Mead and Company, 1950.

The Best Plays of 1950-1951. Edited by John Chapman. Dodd, Mead and Company, 1951.

The Player: A Profile of an Art. Lillian Ross and Helen Ross. Simon and Schuster, 1961.

Great Child Stars. James Robert Parish. Ace Books, 1976.

Sid Caesar: Where Have I Been? Crown Publishers, 1982.

Gram Parsons: A Music Biography. Sid Griffin. Sierra Records. 1985.

I'm With the Band: Confessions of a Groupie. Pamela Des Barres. Beech Tree Books, 1987.

Child Star: An Autobiography. Shirley Temple Black. McGraw Hill, 1988.

Long Time Gone. David Crosby and Carl Gottlieb. Doubleday, 1988.

Hickory Wind: The Life and Times of Gram Parsons. Ben Fong-Torres. St. Martin's Griffin, 1998.

The Making of Shane by Walt Farmer, 2000, www.theastrocowboy.com

Canyon of Dreams: The Magic and Music of Laurel Canyon. Sterling Publishing, 2009.

Breakfast in Nudie Suits. Ian Dunlop. Clarksdale, 2011.

Career Credits

Film

The Member of the Wedding 1952, Columbia Pictures. Directed by Fred Zinnemann, with Ethel Waters and Julie Harris.

Shane 1953, Paramount Pictures. Directed by George Stevens, with Alan Ladd, Van Heflin, and Jean Arthur.

Goodbye My Lady 1956, Warner Brothers. Directed by William A. Wellman, with Walter Brennan and Phil Harris.

Night Passage 1957, Universal Pictures. Directed by James Neilson, with James Stewart, Audie Murphy, and Dan Duryea.

The Missouri Traveler 1958, Warner Brothers. Directed by Jerry Hopper, with Lee Marvin and Gary Merrill.

Blue Denim 1959, Twentieth Century Fox. Directed by Philip Dunne, with Carol Lynley and McDonald Carey.

All Fall Down 1962. Directed by John Frankenheimer, with Warren Beatty, Eva Marie Saint, Karl Malden, and Angela Landsbury.

Hud 1963, Paramount Pictures. Directed by Martin Ritt, with Paul Newman, Melvyn Douglas, and Patricia Neal.

The Tenderfoot 1964, Walt Disney's Wonderful World of Color. Television mini-series. With Brian Keith and James Whitmore.

Those Calloways 1965, Walt Disney. Directed by Norman Tokar, with Brian Keith and Vera Miles.

In Harm's Way 1965, Paramount Pictures. Directed by Otto Preminger, with John Wayne, Kirk Douglas, and Patricia Neal.

The Trip 1967, American International Pictures (AIP). Directed by Roger Corman, with Peter Fonda, Bruce Dern, and Susan Strasberg. Brandon appears as an unbilled extra.

The Deserter 1971, Paramount Pictures. Directed by Burt Kennedy, with Bekim Fehmiu, Richard Crenna, and Chuck Connors.

Wild in the Sky aka Black Jack, 1972, AIP. Directed by William T. Naud with Georg Stanford Brown and Keenan Wynn.

Theater (Broadway)

The Member of the Wedding. Empire Theater. January 5, 1950 to March 17, 1951. With Julie Harris and Ethel Waters.

Mrs. McThing. Martin Beck Theater. February 20, 1952 to January 10, 1953. With Helen Hayes, Lydia Reed, and Ernest Borgnine.

Emperor's Clothes. Ethel Barrymore Theater. February 9, 1953 to February 21, 1953. With Maureen Stapleton, Lee J. Cobb, and John Anderson.

Comes A Day. Ambassador Theater. November 6, 1958 to November 29, 1958. With Judith Anderson, Larry Hagman, and Arthur O'Connell.

Race of Hairy Men! Henry Miller's Theater. April 29,1965 to May 1, 1965. With Martin Huston, Joan McCall, and April Shawhan.

Television

Ed Sullivan Show October 8, 1950 and September 6, 1953.

Philco-Goodyear Television Playhouse No Medals on Pop, 1951; A Cowboy for Chris, 1952.

The Plymouth Playhouse Jamie, 1953.

Jamie (TV series) Twenty-two episodes from "Jamie Tents Out" on October 5, 1953 to second episode of second season, October 4, 1954.

What's My Line? January 10, 1954.

Person to Person January 29, 1954.

The Colgate Comedy Hour March 7, 1954.

Climax! "The Day They Gave Babies Away," December 22, 1955; "An Episode of Sparrows," March 29, 1956.

Star Stage "Bend to the Wind," May 4, 1956.

Screen Director's Playhouse "Partners," July 4, 1956.

The U.S. Steel Hour "The Locked Door," Nov. 6, 1957.

Alcoa Theater "Man of His House," March 9, 1959.

Wagon Train "The Danny Benedict Story," December 2, 1959; "The Mark Miner Story," November 15, 1961.

Thriller "Pigeons from Hell," June 6, 1961.

Alfred Hitchcock Presents "The Sorcerer's Apprentice," January 1, 1962.

The Virginian "50 Days to Moosejaw," December 12, 1962; "The Orchard," October 2, 1968; "Gun Quest," October 21, 1970.

The Doctors and the Nurses "Ordeal," November 14, 1963.

The Greatest Show on Earth "Love the Giver," April 7, 1964.

12 O'Clock High "Here's to Courageous Cowards," December 4, 1964.

The Defenders "The Objector," February 11, 1965.

Combat! "A Sudden Terror," March 29, 1966.

ABC Stage 67 "The Confession," October 19, 1966.

Journey to the Unknown "One on an Island," December 19, 1968.

The Name of the Game "The Bobby Currier Story," February 21, 1969.

Hawaii Five-O "King Kamehameha Blues," November 12, 1969.

Love American Style "Love and the Bachelor," December 22, 1969.

Insight "Confrontation," May 29, 1970.

The Young Rebels "To Hang a Hero," October 11, 1970.

Rod Serling's Night Gallery "Death in the Family," September 22, 1971.

Ironside "In the Line of Duty," October 19, 1971.

Narrative Albums

The Stories of Mark Twain, 1956.
Prokofiev: Peter and the Wolf/ Britten: The Young Person's Guide to the Orchestra. Brandon deWilde is the narrator.